PARALEGAL INTERNSHIP MANUAL

Second Edition

A Student Guide To Career Success

By Charles P. Nemeth, JD, L.L.M.

Copyright © 1995, 1996.
All rights reserved.
Pearson Publications Company
Dallas, Texas.

ISBN 0-929563-32-8

NFPA
SEAL OF EXCELLENCE

ACKNOWLEDGMENT

We thank all those who have contributed to the first edition of this project, but special recognition is extended to Suzanne Sheldon of Woodbury College, Vermont; Tom Williams, John Shaheen, and Laundria Sensabaugh of the American Institute for Paralegal Studies, Southfield, Michigan, and Columbus, Ohio; and Susan Alleman, formerly of Southeastern Paralegal Institute, Dallas, Texas.

We also appreciate the forms and other information contributed by these educational institutions: San Francisco, State College, CA; Mount Vernon Nazarene College, OH; and Saddleback College, CA. Gratitude is especially extended to the author's academic institution, Waynesburg College in Waynesburg, PA, for its generous support. President Timothy Thyreen, vice president Kathleen Davis, and division dean Joseph Graff continue to foster these projects by making college resources available.

We are extremely grateful to editor Carolyn Bullard for her meticulous attention to detail and for polishing the material into a friendly form, both in the first and second editions, and to editors Harriet Dishman and Frances Whiteside for their critical reviews of the first edition.

The author's family, consisting of spouse, Jean Marie and seven children, Eleanor, Stephen, Anne Marie, John, Joseph, Mary Claire, and Michael Augustine, provide the needed impetus for projects of this type.

Charles Nemeth
Author

Enika Pearson Schulze
Publisher

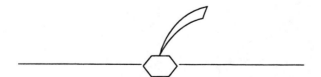

DEDICATION

To Stephen Charles

My first son – kind and decent, strong and gentle, loyal and true.

To Thomas Aquinas

*It is not always through the perfect goodness of virtue that one obeys the law,
but sometimes it is through fear of punishment,
and sometimes from the mere dictate of reason ....*
(Summa Theologica I-II, Question XCII)

Charles P. Nemeth

TABLE OF CONTENTS

Chapter One: Experiential Learning and the Paralegal...................... 1
    Experience and the Educational Method............................ 1
    Defining the Internship.. 4

Chapter Two: The Intern Position... 7
    How to Begin... 7
    Practical Recommendations on Internship Placement.............. 10
    Sample Resumes... 15
    Sample Cover Letters... 19
    Internship Interview.. 24

Chapter Three: Objectives and Goals...................................... 37
    Setting the Stage for an Internship.................................... 37
    Syllabus... 37
    Tracking the Internship Experience.................................... 66
    Measuring Specific Paralegal Traits................................... 74
    Conclusion.. 78

Chapter Four: Ethical Considerations...................................... 81
    The Ethical Framework... 81
    Exercises for the Paralegal Intern..................................... 92
    Conclusion: Finding Your Way Through the Ethical Jungle...... 95

Chapter Five: Role, Tasks, and Obligations.............................. 97
    Stage I: Listen and Observe... 97
    Stage II: Learn by Doing... 98
    Intern Activities.. 102

Chapter Six: The Internship Site... 147
    The Internship Supervisor/Sponsor................................... 149
    Faculty Supervision... 155
    The Sponsoring Organization... 158
    Conclusion... 167

Chapter Seven: Evaluating the Intern Experience....................... 169
    Student Evaluation of the Internship.................................. 169
    Placement Readiness.. 185
    Conclusion... 190

Appendices.. 193
    Appendix A: State Civil Service Centers............................ 193
    Appendix B: Answers to Ethical Queries............................ 199

TABLE OF FIGURES

1-1	Profile of Paralegal Internships	3
2-1	Type of Employer Hiring Paralegals	9
2-2	Resume Worksheet	13
2-3	Sample Resume #1	15
2-4	Sample Resume #2	16
2-5	Sample Resume #3	17
2-6	Sample Cover Letter	19
2-7	Sample Cover Letter	20
2-8	Internship Application #1	21
2-9	Internship Application #2	22
2-10	Internship Cover Letter	22
2-11	Sponsor's Letter of Interest	25
2-12	Intern's Letter of Confirmation	25
2-13	Intern's Letter of Gratitude	29
2-14	Intern's Letter of Nonacceptance	29
2-15	Intern's Letter of Confirmation	34
3-1	Prototypical Syllabus	37
3-2	Description of Internship	40
3-3	Course and Policies of Internship	46
3-4	Checklist of Internship Tasks	47
3-5	Summary of Paralegal Tasks	48
3-6	Grading Policy	62
3-7	Student Responsibilities	63
3-8	Guidelines for a Final Report	64
3-9	Assessment of the Internship Experience	67
3-10	Guidelines for Internship Log	69
3-11	Daily Log Sample	71
3-12	Daily Log Codes	72
3-13	Problem Resolution	74
3-14	Skill Acquisition	75
4-1	Model Standards and Guidelines for Utilization of Legal Assistants	83
4-2	Model Code of Ethics and Professional Responsibility	87
5-1	Sample Assignment	99
5-2	Sample Memo Response	99
5-3	Request for Repairs	104
5-4	Motion for Continuance Worksheet	117
6-1	Responsibilities of the Sponsor	147
6-2	Functions of the Intern	148
6-3	Responsibilities of the Internship Overseer	150
6-4	Letter of Introduction	155
6-5	Request for Midterm Progress Report	156
6-6	Request for Final Evaluation	156
6-7	Status Advisory	157
6-8	Grade/Assignment Database	158
6-9	Operational Design of a Law Firm	161
6-10	Hierarchy of the Department of Justice	162
6-11	Structure of the Veterans Administration	164
7-1	Thank-You Letter to Sponsor from School	185
7-2	Thank-You Letter to Sponsor from the Intern	186
7-3	Thank-You Letter to the Faculty Supervisor from the Intern	187

TABLE OF FORMS

2-1	Preliminary Self-Assessment	10
2-2	List of Potential Sponsors	11
2-3	Steps to the Internship	23
2-4	Evaluation of Interview	28
2-5	Internship Authorization	30
2-6	Internship Authorization	32
2-7	Agreement Between Paralegal Intern and Firm	33
2-8	Indemnification Agreement	35
3-1	Weekly Internship Log	73
3-2	Self-Assessment of Client Counseling Skills	77
5-1	Report on Status of Assignment	100
5-2	Activities Catalog	101
5-3	Client Information Sheet	102
5-4	Checklist for Divorce	105
5-5	Checklist for Agreement of Sale (Buyer's Version)	107
5-6	Checklist for Agreement of Sale (Seller's Version)	110
5-7	Master Mailing List	111
5-8	Settlement Statement	113
5-9	Financial Status	115
5-10	Client Interview for Will Preparation	119
5-11	Corporate Dissolution Checklist	135
5-12	Photography Checklist	137
5-13	Deposition Index	138
5-14	Deposition Log	139
5-15	Outline of Witness Testimony	141
5-17	Sexual Harassment Complaint	142
5-18	Law Library	143
6-1	Supervisor/Sponsor Visitation	151
6-2	Progress Report	152
6-3	Consultation/Observation Charts	153
6-4	Student Evaluation of the Internship Sponsor	154
6-5	Hierarchy of Internship Site	163
6-6	Capital/Income and Expense/Liability Chart	166
7-1	Student Description and Evaluation of Internship Program	170
7-2	Post-Internship Evaluation	171
7-3	Midterm Evaluation	172
7-4	Internship Course Evaluation	173
7-5	Evaluation of Supervisor/Sponsor	174
7-6	Evaluation of Internship Site	175
7-7	Faculty Evaluation of Intern	176
7-8	Midterm Evaluation	178
7-9	Evaluation of Field Studies	179
7-10	Sponsor's Evaluation	181
7-11	Evaluation of Internship	183
7-12	Inventory of Readiness for Job Placement	185
7-13	Student Evaluation	188

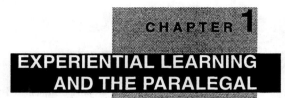

CHAPTER 1
EXPERIENTIAL LEARNING AND THE PARALEGAL

Experience and Educational Method

If you are preparing for a career as a paralegal, this may be your first venture into the working world, or you may have decided to leave one career and start another, or to shift from one specialty to another. However extensive your knowledge of the worlds of business, law, or academia, you are curious about this new field you are entering, and you have many questions about how you can best use your education, your skills, and your life experience as a paralegal. A well-planned internship will help answer your questions and will more than likely be the launching pad for a successful career. Here are some thoughts on the educational process:

Education in the classroom comes in many forms. Students may learn to solve mathematical problems or discuss great thinkers like Aristotle or Socrates. They may analyze and evaluate facts they read in books and exchange ideas. All of these classroom exercises are mental or theoretical, requiring that students obtain information by intellectual association.

While necessary, theoretical learning must be balanced with experience—what a student can observe in the world that lies outside the classroom. Through experiential learning, a student can put classroom theories to the test.

For example, a student who wishes to gauge the Bill of Rights' impact on police search and seizure processes will be able to evaluate the "probable cause" formula during rides in a police car, or during neighborhood drug sweeps, or when working in the prosecutor's office.

It is through experience that people learn how rules of law work in the real world instead of in theory. To be sure, how any theory works in the real world is often forgotten by policy makers, judges, and the academic community.

This may be why some people call academics, college professors, and researchers "eggheads." While this label is contemptuous and unfair, its use is testimony to the rift that exists between those who dream up theories and those who have to apply them. A good example is the antagonism that exists between those who want all prisons demolished and those who want them erected at lightning speed. Some people believe that any prisoner, if loved, can be rehabilitated. Others think all inmates are inherently bad and can never be rehabilitated.

CHAPTER 1

There needs to be a way to close or at least partially bridge this rift between theoreticians and practitioners. Professor Richard Boswell of the University of California urges a clinical experience for all those involved in the law:

> It was Justice Holmes who wrote in 1881 that the law is not simply logic, but experience. The last twenty years have been marked by great tension between those legal educators who believe that coming to a comprehensive understanding of the law is best accomplished through logic and those who maintain it is better acquired through experience. This tension in legal education was manifested in the birth of the modern "clinical" movement.[1]

Boswell sees the roles that theorist/academics and practitioners play as complementary rather than antagonistic. He thinks theoreticians and practitioners should meet halfway.

> The question that we should be asking is whether we are going to be a bridge between the academy and the larger world of lawyers and clients, or whether we will merely inform others in the academy of our own perspectives on law. The roles are quite different. In the former we are communicating amongst all of the groups that shape the law; in the latter we communicate only within the academy. While this need not be an "either/or" proposition, I believe the choice must include providing a bridge between the academy and the larger world. This is the proper choice because we stand in two positions: within the academy, and in the midst of the larger of the law in practice. As active practitioners within the academy, we are uniquely able to contribute to legal education's understanding of the outside world. Each of our constituencies has an important contribution to offer the academy, and we are in an excellent position to talk with and among those constituencies.[2]

The inadequacy of law schools in preparing their students for the real world has prompted the American Bar Association to promulgate a new law school accreditation standard that fosters clinical experiences by making full-time faculty eligible for sabbatical leave. ABA Accreditation Standards 405(e), as enacted, provides that "[t]he law school should afford to full-time faculty whose primary responsibilities are in its professional skills program a form of security of position reasonably similar to tenure and prerequisites reasonably similar to those provided other full-time faculty members."[3]

Although the ABA does not accredit paralegal programs, those legal assistant and paralegal programs whose standards stress an experiential, occupational

EXPERIENTIAL LEARNING AND THE PARALEGAL

tone can receive its voluntary approval. Specifically, the ABA states:

> The institution shall maintain a program for the education of legal assistants that is designed to qualify its graduates to be employed in law-related occupations, including public and private law practice and/or corporate or government law-related activities....The primary concern of a legal assistant education program is to develop occupational competence.[4]

The American Association for Paralegal Education (AAfPE) conducted a survey of paralegal programs that made internships a part of their academic experience with the following results:

Figure 1-1[5]

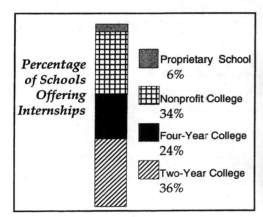

Profile of Paralegal Internships

Type of Institution	Number of Institutions	Number and Percentage of Internships
Two-Year public colleges	35	26 (74%)
Four-Year public colleges and universities	23	17 (77%)
Nonprofit colleges and universities	32	24 (75%)
Proprietary schools	9	4 (44%)

What is most interesting about the AAfPE's survey is how, in a majority of cases, experiential education receives favor in two- and four-year colleges despite the fact that the proprietary emphasis on practicality and vocationalism is often criticized by collegiate educators.

The National Association of Legal Assistants (NALA) advocates experiential learning in its principles as follows:

> Graduation from a course of study for legal assistants..., **plus not less than six months of in-house training as a legal assistant;** A baccalaureate degree in any field, **plus not less than six months in-**

CHAPTER 1

house training as a legal assistant; ... A minimum of three years of law-related experience under the supervision of an attorney, including at least six months of in-house training as a legal assistant; or ... Two years of in-house training as a legal assistant.[6]

Defining the Internship

Precisely how paralegals and legal assistants can blend reality with the abstract is inexorably tied to their opportunity for experiential education. Internships are one of the most commonly used means to this end. An internship is also known as **practicum**, **field work** or **apprenticeship**, and in some circles, **externship**. In *Criminal Justice Internships*, authors Gordon and McBride give the following definition:

"Field work, practicum, and *internship* are used interchangeably to denote either a full- or part-time work experience in which the student is assigned definite tasks and responsibilities. The internship may be a degree requirement, depending on the college's program. Although a monetary stipend is not automatic, the student does earn college credits (or other benefits) the number of which depends on the length of time in the field. The student is required to complete various assignments, as well as the assigned tasks at the field site."[7] The many nuances of these definitional differences are not as important as the basic design of experience-based education.

The structure of the internship experience can be set up in a number of ways. If an educational institution is involved, the simplest structure includes only the school, the intern, and the sponsor — the party or entity allowing the internship experience.

Then again, some internship models may place the bulk of responsibility for the internship program on individual faculty members serving as advisors or supervisors to all interns.

In this context, the faculty member develops the internships, constantly monitors them, and assumes primary responsibility for their operation. Despite these variances, all internship programs have three principal players:

1. the educational entity offering the internship course
2. the student intern
3. the sponsor.

This manual attempts to cover the most typical approaches witnessed in internship programs, even though the terms and conditions of internships vary widely depending upon the institution or program. From preliminary internship

EXPERIENTIAL LEARNING
AND THE PARALEGAL

questionnaires to internship placement, from tracking and logging the internship experience to its various means of evaluation, the manual provides all the necessary tools for the complete internship.

No better mechanism than an internship exists to bridge that gap between the abstract and the concrete, between the classroom and the real world. The internship "lets us see, sometimes unwittingly, what we do not yet know about that world."[8]

Endnotes

1. Richard A. Boswell, *Keeping the Practice in Clinical Education and Scholarship*, 43 Hastings Law J. 1187 (April 1992).
2. Richard A. Boswell, *Keeping the Practice in Clinical Education and Scholarship*, 43 Hastings Law J. 1187, 1192 (April 1992).
3. Richard A. Boswell, *Keeping the Practice in Clinical Education and Scholarship*, 43 Hastings Law J. 1187, 1188 (April 1992); see also Grant H. Morris & John H. Minan, *Confronting the Question of Clinical Faculty Status*, 21 San Diego L. Rev. 793 (1984); see also Stephen F. Befort, *Musings on a Clinic Report: A Selective Agenda for Clinical Legal Education in the 1990s*, 75 Minn. L. Rev. 619, 619 (1991).
4. *Guidelines and Procedures for Obtaining ABA Approval of Legal Assistants Programs,* as amended in 1992.
5. American Association for Paralegal Education, *Summary of Internship Survey Results*, 4 September 1988.
6. The National Association of Legal Assistants, Inc., *Model Standards for Utilization of Legal Assistants Annotated*, 3 (1991).
7. Gary R. Gordon & R. Bruce McBride, *Criminal Justice Internships* 4 (2nd ed. 1990), Anderson Pub. Co.
8. Robert D. Dinerstein, *Clinical Texts and Contexts*, 39 UCLA Law Rev. 697 (1992).

CHAPTER 1

CHAPTER 2
THE INTERN POSITION

How to Begin

"Who wants me?" "Precisely what do I want?" "How do I get what I want?" These are three important questions you must ask yourself as an aspiring intern. You can then develop a plan that will help you identify internship opportunities. To be sure, there are many paths you might follow.

Many institutions have an internship coordinator, director, placement office, or career counseling center entrusted with establishing an internship program. Some have a specific faculty member who aids prospective interns. Both the placement office and the faculty member should have a list of participating sponsors. Because interns' services are beneficial to the sponsoring organization, interns are usually welcomed. Also, other interns and alumni, including recent graduates, are good sources for leads.

An AAfPE internship survey conducted in 1988 produced the following results:

On the question of how internship positions were developed, the vast majority of responses indicated that the positions were developed through personal contacts of the program coordinator, self-placement by the student, or a combination of the two. Other methods of developing internship positions were:
- assistance from an advisory committee
- bar association cooperation
- college placement office
- cooperative education director of college
- federal government cooperation
- full-time career development specialist
- list given to student
- mailings
- referrals from graduates of the program.[1]

Alice Fins' *Opportunities on Paralegal Careers* categorizes opportunities for potential internships in this list:
    Paralegals in the public sector
    — public sector law
    — group legal services
    — legal services corporation
    Paralegals in government
    — the federal government
    — state and local government
    Paralegals in the private sector
    — corporate law
    — estate planning and probate
    — real estate
    — litigation

CHAPTER 2

Nonlawyer court personnel
— court administrators
— counselors and social workers
— data processing specialists
— clerical positions
— court reporters
— security officials
— parajudges
— clerks of the court.[2]

Contact with state and federal civil job centers may be fruitful, as many government agencies, such as the U.S. Department of Justice, have ongoing intern programs. Federal job centers are listed in the white pages under U.S. Government. State civil service centers may also be helpful and are listed in the appendix.

Common sense leads any prospective paralegal intern to the occupational centers in the American legal system. Internships are typically available in the following types of organizations:

law firms
legal service centers
corporate or business legal departments
government agencies
bar and professional associations
law enforcement
courts
judges
hospital legal departments
insurance companies
legal aid and other charitable nonprofit entities
mortgage/title companies
real estate offices.

As you contact potential internship sponsors, you should stress the positive community impact and professional contribution the sponsor will be making. Certainly the history of the legal profession offers a strong precedent for internships. In the 19th century, new lawyers or those seeking admission to the bar had to work with a mentor, usually an experienced lawyer. A mentor's sole purpose was to prepare the novice for the practical realities of lawyering. In those times and, until recently, even in some states, individuals could seek bar admission based on purely practical preparation without study at a law school.

THE INTERN POSITION

Proficiency was measured not merely by law school attendance but by other standards, such as private study or tutoring by mentors who prepared candidates for the bar. In this system of bar admission, older, more experienced lawyers made invaluable contributions to their future colleagues and the profession at large. Modern internships afford the experienced lawyer a similar opportunity, and paralegals are taking a comparable path.

Statistics demonstrate how powerful the law firm environment is for prospective paralegals. According to NALA, more than 50 percent of occupational opportunities for paralegals today are within the law-firm environment (Figure 2-1).

Figure 2-1[3]

Type of Employer Hiring Paralegals

Employer	1991		1993	
	Number	Percent	Number	Percent
Private Law Firm	2045	78%	2392	77%
Bank	20	1%	28	1%
Insurance Company	17	1%	55	2%
Corporation	237	9%	263	8%
Public Sector/Government	125	5%	211	7%
Self-Employed	101	4%	68	2%
Other	92	3%	74	2%

It is not just the large firms that are hiring paralegals. Small or mid-size law firms that hire and use paralegals effectively can increase productivity at a minimum cost. With the increase in prepaid legal plans and the creation of the "superfirm" with branches in several cities, small firms and solo practitioners are under increasing pressure to deliver quality services at a minimum cost. Paralegals can help attorneys in small firms or solo practice meet this challenge.[4]

If you desire a position in a law firm, research the *Martindale-Hubbell Law Directory*, which categorizes lawyers as follows:
- practice index
- corporate law department section
- consultants section
- lawyers in more than 130 countries worldwide

CHAPTER 2

• practice profiles of virtually every attorney in the United States and Canada.

Practical Recommendations on Internship Placement

You should carefully and tactfully present your background to a potential sponsor. You are selling not only the idea of the internship, but also your personality and skills.

By focusing on the targets of your search and where you fit most comfortably, you can narrow the range of options. You can identify yourself as the intern the sponsor should select.

Preliminary Self-Assessment

To determine your specific career interests, use the checklist at Form 2-1 to conduct a preliminary self-assessment.

Form 2-1

Intern Name_____Date_____

Preliminary Self-Assessment

1. Which area of law interests me?_____
2. What are my favorite paralegal activities?_____
3. Why did I decide to apply for an internship?_____
4. What are my expectations regarding field experiences in the program?_____
5. What are my expectations regarding academic experiences in the program?_____
6. What are my expectations regarding professional development in the program?_____
7. How much time and effort will be required of me?_____
8. What do I anticipate this experience will be like?_____
9. How difficult do I think the program will be?_____
10. What will those difficulties be?_____
11. Do I want a paralegal position? If yes, when? _____
12. How will this program help me obtain that position?_____
13. What days of the week and time constraints do I have to consider?_____
14. What benefits will I receive by performing an internship?_____
15. Who do I know who can help me secure an internship?_____
16. What related skills do I need to improve to be an effective intern?_____

Target List

After examining the self-assessment list and analyzing sponsors in your region, chart your ten most desirable targets. Use Form 2-2 to track application and response results.

THE INTERN POSITION

Form 2-2

Intern Name_____ Date_____

List of Potential Sponsors

1. Name of Sponsor _____ Description of
   Address _____ Internship:
   Phone _____ Sponsor Contact _____
   Application Date _____ Response Date_____
   Areas of Practice _____ No. of Paralegals in Firm _____
   Response Results: _____

2. Name of Sponsor _____ Description of
   Address _____ Internship:
   Phone _____ Sponsor Contact _____
   Application Date _____ Response Date_____
   Areas of Practice _____ No. of Paralegals in Firm _____
   Response Results: _____

3. Name of Sponsor _____ Description of
   Address _____ Internship:
   Phone _____ Sponsor Contact _____
   Application Date _____ Response Date_____
   Areas of Practice _____ No. of Paralegals in Firm _____
   Response Results: _____

4. Name of Sponsor _____ Description of
   Address _____ Internship:
   Phone _____ Sponsor Contact _____
   Application Date _____ Response Date_____
   Areas of Practice _____ No. of Paralegals in Firm _____
   Response Results: _____

5. Name of Sponsor _____ Description of
   Address _____ Internship:
   Phone _____ Sponsor Contact _____
   Application Date _____ Response Date_____
   Areas of Practice _____ No. of Paralegals in Firm _____
   Response Results: _____

CHAPTER 2

Form 2-2 (continued)

6. Name of Sponsor _____ Description of
   Address _____ Internship:
   Phone _____ Sponsor Contact _____
   Application Date _____ Response Date _____
   Areas of Practice _____ No. of Paralegals in Firm _____
   Response Results: _____

7. Name of Sponsor _____ Description of
   Address _____ Internship:
   Phone _____ Sponsor Contact _____
   Application Date _____ Response Date _____
   Areas of Practice _____ No. of Paralegals in Firm _____
   Response Results: _____

8. Name of Sponsor _____ Description of
   Address _____ Internship:
   Phone _____ Sponsor Contact _____
   Application Date _____ Response Date _____
   Areas of Practice _____ No. of Paralegals in Firm _____
   Response Results: _____

9. Name of Sponsor _____ Description of
   Address _____ Internship:
   Phone _____ Sponsor Contact _____
   Application Date _____ Response Date _____
   Areas of Practice _____ No. of Paralegals in Firm _____
   Response Results: _____

10. Name of Sponsor _____ Description of
    Address _____ Internship:
    Phone _____ Sponsor Contact _____
    Application Date _____ Response Date _____
    Areas of Practice _____ No. of Paralegals in Firm _____
    Response Results: _____

THE INTERN POSITION

Resume

No internship application will proceed very far without an effective resume. A resume or *vita*, as it is sometimes called, is an abbreviated life summary generally dealing with:

        objectives
        education
        employment history
        references.

Most academic institutions publish resume guides similar to Figure 2-2.

Figure 2-2[5]

Resume Worksheet

Name _____ Date Completed _____
Home address _____
Campus address _____
Job Objective (the job you want) _____

Summary of Qualifications
(why you should be hired)

Education

| College _____
City _____ State _____ Zip _____
Degree _____ Major _____ Minor _____
Expected date of Graduation _____ G.P.A _____
Honors/Awards _____

Other colleges or schools attended:
College _____
City _____ State _____ Zip _____
Degree (if any)_____
Honors/Awards _____ | Other Courses or Seminars
(include city, date) |

Internships/Career Related Experience/Teaching Practicum

| Organization _____
City _____ State _____ Zip _____
Phone _____
Supervisor/Title _____
Date of Employment - From _____ To _____
Job Title _____
Duties/Responsibilities _____
_____ | Accomplishments |

CHAPTER 2

Figure 2-2 (continued)

Employment

	Accomplishments
Organization _____ City _____ State _____ Zip _____ Phone _____ Supervisor/Title _____ Date of Employment - From _____ To _____ Job Title _____ Duties/Responsibilities _____	
Organization _____ City _____ State _____ Zip _____ Phone _____ Supervisor/Title _____ Date of Employment - From _____ To _____ Job Title _____ Duties/Responsibilities _____	Accomplishments
(Please attach additional jobs on a separate sheet)	

Honors/Awards/Special Recognition _____
_____
_____

Campus Activities/Organizations _____
_____
_____

Community Activities _____
_____
_____

Skills and Abilities _____
_____
_____

Volunteer Activities _____
_____
_____

Relevant Courses Taken _____
_____
_____

References

Name _____ Address _____ _____ Work # _____ Home # _____ Occupation/Title _____	Name _____ Address _____ _____ Work # _____ Home # _____ Occupation/Title _____
Name _____ Address _____ _____ Work # _____ Home # _____ Occupation/Title _____	Name _____ Address _____ _____ Work # _____ Home # _____ Occupation/Title _____

**THE INTERN
POSITION**

Most placement experts recommend an abbreviated, clear format for the construction of a resume. Figure 2-3 is a good example.

Figure 2-3

Sample Resume #1

SUSAN P. JONES

Home Address
30-A Carothers Drive
Turtle Creek, PA 15145
412/555-1212

School Address
Box 956, Waynesburg College
Waynesburg, PA 15370
412/555-1213

EDUCATION
WAYNESBURG COLLEGE, Waynesburg, PA 15370
Bachelor of Arts Degree in English with emphasis in Professional Writing
Expected date of Graduation: May 19__

WORK EXPERIENCE
WAYNESBURG COLLEGE, Admissions Office, Waynesburg, PA
Tour Guide/Office Worker (April 1992 to present)
Interact with prospective students and their families. Promote Waynesburg College and help plan visitation days and special events on campus.

K-MART (Edgewood Towne Center), Swissvale, PA
Merchandise Designer (May 1993 to present)
Laid out and designed merchandise; also cashiered.

CHURCH HILL VALLEY COUNTRY CLUB, Penn Hills, PA
Assistant Manager of Pool Shack (Summer 1991, 1992, 1993)
Was party coordinator and purchaser. Was also responsible for employees' work schedules.

ACTIVITIES/ORGANIZATIONS
Student Senate—President, 1994-95; Secretary, 1993-94
Homecoming Director/Coordinator, 1993

COMMUNITY ACTIVITIES
Public Relations Director, St. Colman Fairs
Turtle Creek's 100th Anniversary, Public Relations Assistant

SPECIAL RECOGNITION
Mon Valley's Young Woman of the Year, 1991

RELEVANT COURSES TAKEN
• Business and Technical Writing
• Advertising
• Marketing
• Business and Professional Speaking
• Desktop Publishing

REFERENCES FURNISHED UPON REQUEST

CHAPTER 2

Figure 2-4

Figure 2-4 shows the resume of a person who is changing careers after a long work history in the business world.

Sample Resume #2

Jane P. Story
111 Candy Cane Lane
Atlanta, GA 30303

Work: 404-555-1234   Home: 404-555-1333

Skilled office administrator with 24 years of experience in office administration; excellent administrative, analytical, organizational, and communications skills. A self starter alert to potential problem areas with creative approaches to solutions.

Professional Skills

Administrative
- Administered forms: payment of services; orders for equipment and office supplies; reimbursement of long-distance charges; reimbursement of travel expenses; payroll; computer hardware and software
- Created and summarized reports: financial, statistical data, and human resource
- Drafted and prepared business letters and memos
- Followed up completion for financial reports and appointments to meet deadlines

Analytical
- Analyzed information to resolve errors from Bell Operating Companies and recovered in excess of 4 million dollars
- Analyzed government tariff documentation to communicate with Bell Operating Companies
- Analyzed spreadsheets and improved methodology for submitting information
- Analyzed and developed procedures for recovery of money using on-line computer data

Organizational
- Developed a standard work process and flow in the mailroom that served 400 people
- Developed a uniform filing and tracking system for personnel files for 3 organizations
- Coordinated training and arranged travel accommodations for 3 organizations

Communication
- Coordinated with other business units, all levels of management, and non-management to convert information from manual to computer format

Work History

AT&T

1991-Present	Network Services Division	Reports Clerk
1990	Chief Financial Organization	Reports Clerk
1988	Corporate Human Resources	Reports Clerk

Mountain Bell

1969-1982	Clerk, Equipment Chief

Computer Systems
Software: Microsoft Windows (Word, Excel); Ami Pro
Systems: Basic UNIX, VI Editor

Education
Paralegal Certificate, February 1995
Associate Degree of Applied Science

THE INTERN
POSITION

A third resume example is at Figure 2-5.

Figure 2-5

Sample Resume #3

JOHN Q. SMITH

P.O. Box 683
Waynesburg, PA 15370
(412) 627-8636

OBJECTIVE: An administrative position using my research, planning, and communication skills.

QUALIFICATIONS: Capable in all areas of research. Proven planning, analytical, and organizational skills. Demonstrated excellent communication skills, both written and interpersonal.

ACHIEVEMENTS: **Researched** federal, state, and case law that was used for legal cases, educational texts, publications, and legal analysis papers.

Designed modifications to existing Public Service Administration Program at Waynesburg College, utilizing TV technology to be consistent with the Annenberg Corporation for Public Broadcasting Guidelines.

Completed research and analyzed data for Seat Belt Safety Grant Proposal adhering to required schedule and guidelines. The grant was funded in the amount of $64,000.

Demonstrated analytical and writing skills in legal analysis papers and grant proposals.

Organized a resource library for Waynesburg College Public Service Administration students. Involved identifying and cataloging over 300 legal and research volumes.

Conducted thorough inquiries into constituent concerns while interning for the Honorable H. William DeWeese, Majority Leader, State House of Representatives. This resulted in satisfactory resolution of most problems.

Planned most aspects of Waynesburg College homecoming parades for three years, the largest in approximately 10 years.

Recruited senators for Waynesburg College Student Senate, while president and recording secretary, to provide the largest membership in 10 years.

CHAPTER 2

Figure 2-5 (continued)

Sample Resume #3

Qualified for Dean's List 6 out of 8 semesters by earning 3.30+ or 3.5 grade point averages.

Restructured and edited student body constitution and bylaws.

EXPERIENCE:

Clerical/research assistant
Public Service Administration
Waynesburg College, Waynesburg, PA
Charles P. Nemeth, Director

Constituent liaison intern
State House of Representatives
Waynesburg, PA
Honorable H. William DeWeese
Majority Leader

Residential program worker
Twin Trees, Inc.
Connellsville, PA

Tour guide
Admissions Office
Waynesburg College, Waynesburg, PA

EDUCATION:
Bachelor of Arts 1995
Waynesburg College, Waynesburg, PA

COMPUTER SKILLS:

WordPerfect 5.1	Lotus 1-2-3
Excel	Apple Spreadsheet

HONORARY ACHIEVEMENTS:
Who's Who Among Students in American Universities and Colleges
Alpha Phi Sigma Criminal Justice Honor Society
Senior Public Service Administration Departmental Honors
Waynesburg College Scholarship

Here are some other important suggestions for preparing a resume:

1. A resume must be typed or prepared on a word processing program without typographical or grammatical errors.
2. A resume should seldom exceed one page.
3. A resume should present a pleasant, eye-catching format.
4. A resume must include all relevant work experience.
5. A resume must be updated periodically as accomplishments and career circumstances change.
6. A resume should be typed or printed on high-quality paper. It .... should be mailed with a cover letter in a matching envelope. (White, ivory, and grey are all acceptable colors.)

The cover letter should be concise and identify your job preference. It affords the reader easy access to your address and telephone number. A well-written cover letter provides a unique opportunity for you, as applicant, to make your resume stand out from others. A typical cover letter is shown in Figure 2-6.

Figure 2-6

Sample Cover Letter

105 Broadbrook Drive   October 5, 19__
City, OH 23456
(614) 555-5910

Mr. Henry Blanc
Reid, Rubowitz, and Blanc
2222 Lawyers Way
Suite 8
Rightplace, OH 24033

Dear Mr. Blanc:

I am a senior at Remsen College, majoring in Paralegal Studies. At this time I am seeking an internship placement during the spring semester. Ms. Amber Grantan of our Paralegal Department informed me that you have accepted interns from Remsen College in the past.

Because yours is one of the premier firms in the city, I am very interested in an internship there. My resume is enclosed. You will notice that I have a high grade point average.

Please let me know if you or someone in your department could interview me. I look forward to hearing from you at your earliest convenience.

Sincerely,

Ruby Nicholson

CHAPTER 2

Placement Office Documentation	Placement offices or internship coordinators may have various forms or documents that need preparation before an internship can begin. Check with your internship or placement coordinator for the required filings.
Internship Application	Typically, an explanatory cover letter accompanies the application package. See See Figure 2-7 for an example.

Figure 2-7

Sample Cover Letter

Dear Internship Applicant:

So that we may better assist you in arranging internship opportunities for the next semester, please complete the enclosed information form. It will help us ensure that you are interviewing in a work environment that will help you attain your educational and career goals.

We also require that you keep a journal of your daily experiences with samples of the work product produced for evaluation purposes.

You may already have your internship arrangements made for next semester. If you have made any agreements with a sponsor who is not in the program, your sponsor needs to fill out an information form.

We must approve all internships prior to their start. The normal application process for students is as follows:

1. Fill out and return the information form to this office.
2. Begin interviews after our internship orientation session.
3. Once interviews are completed and internships are secured, you must notify us so we can approve your placement.
4. We must receive a contract letter from your sponsor.

Sincerely,

Internship Coordinator

Figure 2-8 is an example of an Internship Application from Mount Vernon Nazarene College.

20

THE INTERN POSITION

Figure 2-8

Internship Application #1

Mount Vernon Nazarene College
Application for Admission into the Senior Internship Program
Return to Major Department Head by March 1

1.   Name [ ] Miss
             [ ] Mrs. _____
             [ ] Mr.

2.   College or Local Address _____
          _____
          _____

3.   Local Telephone _____ Age _____

4.   Circle the term you wish to participate in the internship program.

        Summer   Fall   January   Spring   Year _____

5.   Number of credit hours completed (include the current term). _____
          Cumulative Grade Point Average _____
          First Major _____GPA _____
          Second Major _____GPA _____
          First Minor _____GPA _____
          Second Minor _____GPA _____

6.   First choice of type of internship placement (e.g., advertising in a retail store, social work in an abuse shelter, etc.) _____
          _____

          Second choice of type of internship placement_____
          _____

7.   Describe the duties/responsibilities you prefer to perform in your internship placement. _____
          _____
          _____

8.   Curriculum area and number of credit hours desired in the internship (e.g., BSS524, SOC523, etc.)
          _____

9.   Describe your work commitment and course load during the internship period. _____
          _____
          _____

10.   Describe any health condition which might hinder or limit the type of responsibilities permitted or assigned during the internship placement. _____
          _____
          _____

11.   Describe the type of transportation available to you during the internship. _____
          _____
          _____

12.   Academic Advisor's Name _____

13.   Student Signature _____ Date_____

14.   Department Action _____ Date_____

CHAPTER 2

Another variation is the Student Application for Internship appearing in Figure 2-9.

Figure 2-9

Internship Application #2

Date: _____ Name: _____ Address: _____
Name of Proposed Internship Supervisor: _____ Name of Company/Firm/Organization
(if applicable) : _____ Principal location where internship will be conducted:_____
Description of facility(ies) to be used: (Include physical layout, monitoring arrangement, type and model
of instrument(s) utilized.) _____
I hereby agree to abide by all promulgated rules, regulations, policies, and requirements applicable to the
completion of this internship.

(Intern Applicant Signature) _____

Placement
Cover Letter

Some educational institutions provide student interns with a cover letter and internship description sent in conjunction with the intern's resume. In the example below (Figure 2-10), sponsors are introduced to the academic institution and the prospective intern.

Figure 2-10

Internship Cover Letter

March 21, 19__

RE: Internship Program

Dear _____ :

I would like to take the opportunity to present to you the American Institute for Paralegal Studies, Inc. convenient and cost-free Internship Program.

The Internship Program provides the opportunity for our students and graduates to gain on-the-job paralegal experience in order to increase their effectiveness in the legal environment. The Internship is mandatory for all students. I am enclosing information regarding this program so you can consider the opportunity of becoming an internship sponsor.

The American Institute has been teaching its course of study since 1978. Our graduates can be found in Fortune 500 companies, Big Six accounting firms, and major law firms throughout the United States. The success of our graduates can be attributed to three major factors:
1. The students tend to be mature, working adults with significant college and/or work experience.
2. We have a comprehensive curriculum and experienced faculty.
3. We are committed to ongoing and professional placement assistance for our students and our graduates.

(continued)

THE INTERN POSITION

Figure 2-10 (continued)

As Internship Coordinator for the American Institute, I work closely with our students assessing their skills and abilities. Because of this, I am able to pre-screen the resumes and select only those candidates whose skills meet the needs of the sponsor.

If you have additional questions about the program, please feel free to contact the Placement Office for further assistance. Thank you for your attention to the American Institute's Internship Program. I look forward to assisting you!

Most sincerely,

Internship Coordinator

Armed with a target list, a resume, a cover letter, and other internship documentation, you should be ready to begin your research. Be aware of all possible strategies for landing an internship by using the checklist, *Steps to the Internship*, in Form 2-3.

Form 2-3

Intern Name_____Date_____

Steps to the Internship

As a paralegal intern, you should:

1. Identify the type of legal environment in which you want to work.
2. Check for possibilities within your network. Talk to other students or working paralegals.
3. Use the *Martindale-Hubbell* directory, the telephone book, and other sources to identify .... firms and organizations in your geographic area.
4. Check your institution's placement office for leads.
5. Contact firms/agencies to inquire about internship possibilities.

If you call, you should:

1. Identify yourself as a paralegal student.
2. Explain that you are looking for an internship, that you need a certain number of hours, and that this type of law practice interests you.
3. Ask if a meeting can be arranged to discuss internship possibilities. If so, schedule an appointment.
4. Notify the intended sponsor of information that should be given to the placement office (or other responsible office).

(continued)

CHAPTER 2

Form 2-3 (continued)

If you write, you should:

1. Direct the cover letter to a specific individual.
2. Identify yourself as a paralegal student.
3. Explain that you are looking for an internship, that you need a certain number of hours, and that this type of law practice interests you.
4. Mention any background skills or experience that would complement the setting.
5. State that additional information is available through your school's placement office (or other responsible office).
6. Schedule an interview with the intended intern supervisor. Take your resume to the meeting.

You should discuss the following topics at the interview:

1. Work schedule for completing required hours.
2. The sponsor's practice and office decorum.
3. The sponsor's expectations and any policies concerning the internship relationship.
4. Supervision: Ask the sponsor who your direct supervisor will be.
5. Job responsibilities and minimum performance level.
6. Time to be allocated to various internship tasks.
7. Confidentiality. Inform the supervisor that he or she is required to complete a daily log and final report, which will include, if possible, copies of work product (with any confidential information blocked out).
8. Other ethical standards including client confidentiality, conflict of interest, legal advice, attorney supervision.
9. Any special reading assignments the sponsor might require before you begin the internship.

Be certain you complete all necessary paperwork for your sponsor or institution.

Internship Interview

An intern's application is not usually accepted and approved without a face-to-face meeting. Both the sponsor and the educational institution should require an interview to assure a long-term and satisfactory relationship between student and sponsor. Generally, the sponsoring agency will correspond with the intern regarding an interview as follows in Figure 2-11:

THE INTERN POSITION

Figure 2-11

Sponsor's Letter of Interest

Mary Smith
Clearbrook Paralegal School
Clearbrook, IA 52216

May 8, 19__

Dear Ms. Smith:

I have received your letter requesting an internship with our firm. I find your credentials acceptable and would like you to attend an interview on Tuesday, May 23, at 10 a.m. in my office.

I look forward to meeting you. If you have any questions prior to the 23rd, do not hesitate to call.

Sincerely,

Jay Filburn, Director
Wynona County Legal Aid

As a courtesy and a sign of professionalism, you should formally draft a note of thanks confirming the time and place of the interview. See Figure 2-12 for a sample response.

Figure 2-12

Intern's Letter of Confirmation

Jay Filburn, Director
Wynona County Legal Aid
222 Read Street
Clearbrook, IA 52208

May 10, 19__

Dear Mr. Filburn:

I would be happy to be interviewed on Tuesday, May 23, at 10 a.m. in your office. Thank you for this wonderful opportunity. I look forward to meeting you.

Sincerely,

Mary Smith

CHAPTER 2

The Interview

Actual interviews can be thoroughly unpredictable events. However, you can be best prepared for the interview by heeding the following suggestions:

Know Your Interviewer

Whether you are interviewing at a law firm, a corporation, or a government agency, know something about the person conducting the interview. There is nothing wrong with gathering information from employees, other firms in contact with the intended sponsor, or third parties who may have knowledge of the interviewer. Remember, if you are going to be interviewed for an internship in a law firm, use *Martindale-Hubbell* or other professional directories like those of the American Bar Association or the Association of Trial Lawyers of America. Other helpful resources include:

- LEXIS/NEXIS
- information services such as Information America and DIALOG
- Standard and Poor's
- Moody's
- regional trade papers
- bar association magazines and newsletters
- colleagues
- placement agencies
- *Legal Assistant Today* magazine
- Dun and Bradstreet
- annual reports
- local newspapers and magazines
- articles in local business journals
- former employees.[9]

Dress Professionally

The legal community is rather conservative, at least in the fashion context. Gaudy, loud, or bizarre clothing creates an unfavorable impression. Students learn quickly that most agencies and firms expect interns to wear traditional business clothes. In fact, courts and judges tend to demand it. Some suggestions are as follows:

DO NOT WEAR
> bold colors
> exotic perfumes, colognes, or makeup
> unconventional haircuts
> outrageous jewelry

DO WEAR/TAKE
> reasonable shoe design
> modest hems
> clean, pressed, businesslike clothes
> traditional attache or briefcase.

THE INTERN POSITION

Be On Time

Tardiness destroys opportunities. "Better late than never" is a useless maxim in internship circles. Allow extra time to arrive at a destination in case of car trouble or busy traffic. Anything can happen! Being timely allows the mind and body to settle, relax, and prepare for the experience without being rushed or tense.

Be Assertive, Not Aggressive

You do not want to give the impression you are docile and manipulable during the interview. Neither do you want to be aggressive. Be attentive, alert, prepared, and not afraid to ask questions. The sponsor will respect your wanting to know all aspects of the internship. Prepare a short list of questions ahead of time. Alter your list based on information you learn during the interview. Here are some ideas:

- Can you describe a typical day for the paralegal intern position?
- To whom do paralegal interns report?
- Are paralegals considered part of the support staff or part of the professional staff?
- Can you give me examples of types of assignments I will be expected to perform?
- Is travel involved?
- What kind of client contact, if any, is involved?
- What is the firmwide ratio of attorneys to paralegals? Partners to associates?
- What type of computer system (hardware and software) does the firm use?
- How many attorneys is each paralegal assigned to in this department?
- Can you give me a brief history of the firm? When did the firm first utilize paralegals?
- How will I receive my assignments?
- What access will I have to the library/forms/LEXIS/WESTLAW?
- Do paralegal interns in this firm/company perform legal research?
- How many offices does the firm or company have and where are they located? Is this a branch office?[10]

It is standard practice for a decision on intern selection to be announced at a later date. You should ask how you will be advised of any decision.

Interview Evaluation

After the interview, write down your impression of the experience. Did the interview prompt further interest? Are you fully aware of all terms, conditions, duties, tasks, and responsibilities associated with the internship? Did you feel comfortable with the sponsor or supervisor? Is this the type of work environment you want? An evaluation document that asks these questions is reproduced at Form 2-4.

27

CHAPTER 2

Form 2-4

Intern Name_____Date_____

Evaluation of Interview

Firm/Company: _____Address: _____
Date of Interview: _____Interviewed with: _____
Title: _____Thank-you letter sent: _____

1. My initial reaction was:
   Must intern here___   Seems appealing___   Need more info___   Not sure___
   Warning flag___

2. I enjoyed meeting the interviewer:
   Yes___   Somewhat___   Felt intimidated___   This was not the person who
   would supervise me___

3. How clearly did the interviewer describe the internship responsibilities?
   Very clearly___   Somewhat clearly___   Not clearly at all___

4. To what extent will this position meet my internship criteria and goals?
   Exactly what I want___   May meet my goals___   Not sure___   Will not meet___

5. I understand the firm/company's culture and attitudes toward legal assistants:
   Very clearly___   Somewhat clearly___   Not clearly at all___

6. What I would like from this position is: _____

7. What excites me about this position is: _____

8. What concerns me about this position is: _____

9. I have discussed this internship position with my network/colleagues/mentor or board of advisors:
   _____

10. I would like to pursue this internship position:
    Yes___   No___   Worth thinking about___

Interview
Follow-up

No matter what the result of the interview, courtesy demands a thank-you letter expressing gratitude for the opportunity to visit and discuss the internship (Figure 2-13).

THE INTERN POSITION

Figure 2-13

Intern's Letter of Gratitude

January 3, 19—

Mrs. Lena Allen
Travis and Allen
21 Church Street
Junction Gap, CO 80289

Dear Mrs. Allen:

Thank you for the opportunity to meet with you today for an internship interview. I appreciate your time and consideration.

The topics we discussed and the questions you answered for me reinforce my interest in the experiences offered. In addition, I believe your firm could benefit from my skills and knowledge.

I look forward to hearing from you.

Sincerely,

Susan Jones

If you want to decline an offer, you can write a letter similar to the one in Figure 2-14.

Figure 2-14

Intern's Letter of Nonacceptance

April 2, 19—

Ms. Marina Randolph
Beacon County Courthouse
Beaconville, TX 75345

Dear Ms. Randolph:

Thank you for your interest in me for your internship position. While your offer would provide a wonderful opportunity, unfortunately I must decline.

After much consideration, I have decided I would benefit more from a position in a different area of law. I greatly appreciate your time and consideration.

Sincerely,

Lawrence Riley

CHAPTER 2

Internship Agreements

Formal documentation evidences the agreement between sponsor and intern. The intern and sponsor should formalize their arrangement with a legal document such as an Internship Authorization document (Form 2-5). The parties make promises and are signatories.

Form 2-5

Intern Name_____Date_____

Internship Authorization

Intern's Name _____ Student I.D.# _____

Supervisor's Name _____ Title_____

Firm Name, Address _____

_____

Phone Number _____

INTERN'S EMPLOYMENT SCHEDULE

Internship starting date _____Internship completion date _____

Days of the week and hours per day _____

Area of practice/area of law _____

Job description/required duties _____

Knowledge and skills the intern expects to acquire _____

_____

As an internship sponsor, I, _____ ,agree to:

1. Provide appropriate supervision to the intern at all times.
2. Assign meaningful work experience.
3. Ensure that sufficient equipment and/or materials are available to complete work assignments.
4. Provide the intern with instructions necessary to succeed in this position.
5. Reimburse the intern for expenses incurred while performing work for this office.
6. Review the intern's daily log.

THE INTERN POSITION

Form 2-5 (continued)

    7. Hold one conference with the intern each week, or at least each month.

    8. Complete the sponsor's evaluation at the end of the internship and review the evaluation with the intern.

As an intern, I, _____ , agree to:

    1. Abide by the sponsor's rules and regulations regarding employment.

    2. Complete the daily log and final report describing the internship experience.

    3. Submit the daily log, final report, and sponsor's evaluation to the internship coordinator at the end of the internship.

    4. Respect the confidentiality of information pertaining to the sponsor's business, including client names and subject matter of their legal concerns. Copies of my work product will be retained with the permission of the sponsor; however, proper names will be removed or redacted. Copies of particularly sensitive documents will not be retained.

The internship and commensurate responsibilities described above are understood and agreed upon by both the intern and the supervisor.

Supervisor's Signature _____ Date _____

Intern's Signature _____ Date _____

Only when a supervisor or sponsor offers a position can the intern seek applicable institutional or faculty approval. Some faculty or instructors devise a Learning Contract such as Form 2-6.

CHAPTER 2

Form 2-6

Intern Name_____Date_____

Internship Authorization

Part I.

A. Name
Social Security No.
Campus Address
Home Address
Address while on internship

B. Internship Organization
Address
Telephone
Name of Supervisor
Position
Your position

C. Faculty Sponsor/Advisor
Department
Address
Telephone

D. Credits to be awarded for internship

Department
Course No.   No. of Credits

Part II. The Internship

A. Job Description: Describe in as much detail as possible your role and responsibilities while on your internship. List duties, projects to be completed, deadlines, etc., if relevant.

B. Supervision: Describe in as much detail as possible the supervision to be provided. What kind of instruction, assistance, consultation, etc., you will receive and from whom, etc.

C. Evaluation: How will your work performance be evaluated? By whom? When?

Part III. Learning Objectives/Learning Activities/Evaluation

A. Learning Objectives: What do you intend to learn through this experience? Be Specific. Try to use concrete, measurable terms.

B. Learning Activities: 1.   On-the-job: Describe how your internship activities will enable you to meet
your learning objectives.
2.   Off-the-job: List any other activity you will participate in which will help
you   meet learning objectives.

C. Evaluation: How will you know what you have learned, or that you have achieved your learning objectives?

Part IV. Agreement

This contract may be terminated or amended by student, faculty sponsor or internship supervisor at any time upon written notice, which is received and agreed to by the other two parties.

Student Signature _____ Date _____
Faculty Sponsor _____ Date _____
Internship Sponsor _____ Date _____

THE INTERN POSITION

This document centralizes information on all the parties, from intern to supervisor, and their respective obligations.

You may be asked to complete an Internship Agreement that delineates agency and paralegal responsibilities. A sample is at Form 2-7.

Form 2-7[13]

Intern Name_____Date_____

**Agreement Between
Paralegal Intern and Firm**

This agreement acknowledges the importance of the internship. The intent of this agreement is to assure you of our deep appreciation of your services and to indicate our commitment to do the very best we can do to make your experience a productive and rewarding one.

I. <u>Firm</u>

We, _____ (Firm), agree to accept the services of _____ _____ (Student) beginning _____ , and we commit to the following:

1. To provide adequate information, training, and assistance for the intern to be able to meet the responsibilities of the position.
2. To ensure that a supervisor be appointed to aid interns in performing their tasks and to provide feedback on their performance.
3. To respect the skills, dignity and individual needs of the intern and to do our best to adjust to these individual requirements.
4. To be receptive to any comments from the intern regarding ways in which we might better accomplish our respective tasks.
5. To treat the intern as an equal partner with our staff, jointly responsible for completion of paralegal tasks.
6. To provide meaningful paralegal tasks that will facilitate a productive experiential learning experience.
7. To provide a safe working environment and all tools necessary to complete the task.
8. To complete and return attached job description with this agreement prior to the intern's start date.

(continued)

CHAPTER 2

Form 2-7 (continued)

II. <u>Intern</u>

I, _____, agree to serve as a paralegal intern and commit to the following:

1. To perform my paralegal duties to the best of my ability.
2. To adhere to the firm's rules and procedures including recordkeeping requirements and confidentiality of firm and client information.
3. To meet time and duty commitments, or to provide adequate notice so that alternative ....
   arrangements can be made.

III. <u>Schedule of Hours</u>

Monday _____   Thursday _____
Tuesday _____   Friday _____
Wednesday _____   Saturday _____

IV. <u>Signed:</u>

(Intern)_____ (Date) _____
(Agency Representative) _____ (Date) _____

This agreement may be canceled at any time at the discretion of either party but will expire on _____ unless renewed. Any questions or concerns can be addressed by calling

_____.

A placement officer or internship coordinator must approve the internship arrangement. If acceptable, the institution should advise the student in writing (Figure 2-15).

Figure 2-15[14]

Intern's Letter of Confirmation

RE: Internship Authorization

Dear_____:

Thank you for submitting your intern authorization form. Congratulations on your success in finding an intern position. We hope the intern experience enhances your classroom training and assists you in becoming a more valuable paralegal.

Based on our review of your authorization form, your sponsor, job description, and schedule have been approved. You may begin your internship.

(continued)

THE INTERN
POSITION

Figure 2-15 (continued)

Attached are additional copies of the internship log guidelines, daily log (which you will need to photocopy for each day of the internship), final report guidelines, and your mid-internship evaluation (which you will please submit by _____). If you have any questions, please feel free to call the placement department.

We wish you much luck and success as you proceed to complete your internship experience.

Sincerely,

Internship Coordinator _____ Placement Director _____

Some sponsors may wish to have an Indemnification Agreement for protection in case of an accident. See Form 2-8.

Form 2-8

Intern Name_____Date_____

Indemnification Agreement

Dear _____:

The [Name of Educational Institution], [Name of Intern], in consideration of [Name of Internship Sponsor] providing facilities, equipment, and staff for the conduct of intern training experience at [location], in the field of_____ , for [Name of Intern], during the period_____ to_____ under the mutual cooperation, direction, and supervision of the [Name of Educational Institution] and _____ , does hereby agree to defend, hold harmless, indemnify, and release [Name of Internship Sponsor] from and against all claims, demands and actions, or causes of action, for damage to personal property, personal injury, or death which may directly result from the negligence of the [Name of Educational Institution] and [Name of Intern], its officers, employees, and agents.

If this indemnification is satisfactory, please acknowledge your acceptance by signing the attached copy and returning it to my attention.

Sincerely,   ACCEPTED:

(Educational Institution)_____   (Internship Sponsor) _____

(Printed name) _____   (Printed name) _____

(Date) _____   (Date) _____

35

CHAPTER 2

Once your internship agreement has been finalized, consider the goals and objectives outlined in Chapter Three. You will want to keep these in mind as you consider the ethical guidelines in Chapter Four.

Endnotes

1. American Association for Paralegal Education, Summary of Internship Survey Results 9 (1988).
2. Alice Fins, *Opportunities in Paralegal Careers* 8-9 (1990). VGM Career Books: Lincolnwood, IL.
3. National Association of Legal Assistants, 1516 S. Boston, Ste 200, Tulsa, OK 74119. This table originally appeared in the 1993 National Utilization and Compensation Survey Report for the Legal Assistant Profession.
4. Deborah A. Howard, Using Paralegals in Small and Mid-Size Law Firms, 5 *Journal of Paralegal Education & Practice* 67, 68 (1988); see also Nancy L. Helmich & Roger A. Larson, Legal Assistants in Public Law: Their Role in Attorney Generals' Offices, 5 *Legal Assistant Update* 67 (1986).
5. Waynesburg College, Waynesburg, PA 15370.
6. Mount Vernon Nazarene College, Mount Vernon, OH 43050.
7. American Institute for Paralegal Studies, Inc., Southfield, MI 48075.
8. American Institute for Paralegal Studies, Inc., Southfield, MI 48075.
9. Chere B. Estrin, *The Paralegal Career Guide*, 207-08 (1992). Wiley Law Publications: New York.
10. Chere B. Estrin, *The Paralegal Career Guide*, 217-18 (1992). Wiley Law Publications: New York.
11. Chere B. Estrin, *The Paralegal Career Guide*, 222-24 (1992). Wiley Law Publications: New York.
12. American Institute for Paralegal Studies, Inc., Southfield, MI 48075.
13. Waynesburg College, Waynesburg, PA 15370.
14. American Institute for Paralegal Studies, Inc., Southfield, MI 48075.

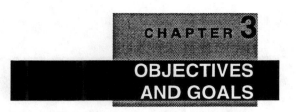

CHAPTER 3
OBJECTIVES AND GOALS

Setting the Stage for an Internship

Now that you have acquired an internship position, you must set out specific objectives:
- What do you expect to gain from the internship?
- What benefits, either personal or occupational, can be achieved?
- What can you reasonably expect to do and accomplish during this introductory phase in your life as a paralegal?
- What do you expect to learn during the internship?
- What are your placement prospects once you complete the internship?
- What type of assignments or academic requirements are called for during the internship?

Any well-managed internship will provide sufficient instruction on these, as well as other relevant questions. From the syllabus and internship description, you should evaluate your internship opportunity in light of what has been promised.

Syllabus

Consider the syllabus for a field experience/internship class available at San Francisco State University shown at Figure 3-1.

Figure 3-1[1]

Prototypical Syllabus

San Francisco State University
Extended Education Paralegal Studies Program

FALL SEMESTER
The goal of this class is to assist paralegal students in bridging the gap between the classroom and the world of legal offices, corporations, public agencies, and organizations -- the legal assistant's "work world."

A group advising session is held at the beginning of the semester to help students find placements in their area of legal interest. Students may solicit their own placements, or arrange special placements with their current employer. All placements **must be approved by the instructor before students begin working at a particular placement.**

CHAPTER 3

Figure 3-1 (continued)

After the advising session, you are required to:

Contact possible placement persons and arrange for an interview with your potential supervisor. Be sure to bring your resume and a writing sample (if requested) to your interview. Interviews should be scheduled no later than two weeks after the advising session to allow maximum time to complete your required hours of work.

Draft a letter of agreement that sets out in specific detail your days and hours of work, your duties, and the requirements of this course (journal and sample work product). Explain to your supervisor that all work products will be sanitized to protect the confidential nature of the document.

Send one copy of your letter of agreement to: **instructor** at _____ by ___/___/___ or earlier. Retain a copy of this letter for your reference to insure that you are working at appropriate and agreed upon paralegal tasks and not simple clerical tasks.

You may begin working at your placement as soon as your placement is approved by the instructor. You are required to work ___ hours during the ___ week semester. Days and hours of work are flexible and depend on individual arrangements.

COURSE REQUIREMENTS
Students are required to attend **all monthly seminars**, and to keep a journal that shall include dates and hours worked, a specific description of the project or task, and a sample of the written work product. Samples should be sanitized for privacy of persons and the confidential nature of the document. Public-record information need not be sanitized. You may also include a section for your own personal comments and observations of your work environment, any problems encountered in completing that project, etc.

Supervising attorneys, legal assistants, and/or office managers are expected to complete midterm and final evaluation forms, which will be mailed to them at appropriate times. Students are encouraged to set up interviews with their supervisors to discuss evaluations and **should receive copies of their completed evaluation forms.**

COURSE MATERIALS
Selected reading materials from professional journals and legal periodicals will be duplicated by the instructor and provided to students at a cost to be determined. Students are expected to read those articles pertinent to each seminar topic **in advance** of the seminar and to be prepared to discuss those readings at the seminar. Students are encouraged to bring additional articles of interest to class for discussion.

SEMINARS
Dates for this semester are:
Dates are subject to change, but every effort will be made to maintain these dates. All seminars will be held at_____ room. Seminar hours are_____to_____. Each seminar will begin with a

OBJECTIVES AND GOALS

Figure 3-1 (continued)

roundtable discussion of each student's work experience — allowing time for students to share concerns and discuss problems. Students with "work problems" often find suggestions and helpful hints from other students who may have worked through similar situations.

Each seminar will focus on a topic specific to the work world of the legal assistant.

GRADING POLICY
Pass, Credit, or Noncredit — no letter grade
Seminar participation — 20 percent
Journal completion — 20 percent
Evaluation of supervisor — 60 percent

SEMINAR TOPICS
SEMINAR ONE
Paralegal ethics, conflicts of interest, NFPA *Model Code of Ethics and Professional Responsibility*, 1991 Judge Chiantelli case, law firm disqualification, checking for conflicts.

SEMINAR TWO
Interpersonal communication in the legal work world — active listening techniques. Adapting communication style to attorney personality type, positive approaches to improving communication, role-play demonstrations.

SEMINAR THREE
Time- and priority-management techniques — stress management tips. Educating attorneys in efficient use of paralegal talent; building respect as an assertive professional; stress busters; and working smarter, not harder.

SEMINAR FOUR
Office politics — negotiating instead of griping, understanding the particular work culture, and adapting to unwritten role-model expectations.

Other professional development topics will be discussed as they relate to bridging the gap from student to professional legal assistant. Students will also give a brief oral report on the benefits of their placements and what they learned on the job.

The San Francisco model, above, includes a discussion of course content, requirements, materials, and grading policy. By reading the syllabus closely, potential interns can glean reasonable expectations about what is to come.

Much can be learned, as well, by studying the internship description offered by Mount Vernon Nazarene College, Mount Vernon, Ohio. The goals, learning outcome, course requirements, and other policies of this program are shown in Figure 3-2.

CHAPTER 3

Figure 3-2[2]

Description of Internship

The internship is a supervised experience normally performed off campus in a professional environment representing a student's major discipline. The student usually devotes forty hours to the cooperating organization for each semester hour of credit earned. If the student is already employed by the organization sponsoring the internship, the supervisory responsibility is assigned to new areas beyond those required in employment. Students are placed in organizations that can provide learning experience and supervision, and in which the student can provide contributions to the organization.

Internship: A supervised experience is performed in a professional environment representing a student's major discipline. Prerequisite: senior standing and departmental application and approval.

Internship Goals
The college has established the following instructional goals for internships:

1. To provide the student with a meaningful, practical experience in a professional setting.
2. To assist the student in clarifying career goals and to assess readiness to enter a chosen profession.
3. To provide the student an opportunity to refine professional skills.
4. To assist the student in integrating the ethical requirements of the workplace with his or her own ethical heritage.

Internship Application
and Placement Procedure
Since the internship experience is a structured educational experience outside the campus, college personnel must supervise and oversee the experience while relying on the sponsoring organization for assistance. The application and placement procedure involves the following steps:

1. During the junior year, a prospective intern secures an internship application from the major department. The completed internship application and a resume are submitted together no later than March 1 for placement during the following summer or academic year. The Career Center staff can provide guidance and models to the student for writing a resume, at the student's request.

2. Between March 1 and the spring preregistration period in April, departmental faculty meet to review departmental internship applications. The department votes to approve or deny each applicant. The department head communicates, in writing, the departmental vote to the student.

3. If the internship is approved, the prospective intern enters the internship course number on the preregistration form during the preregistration period for the following academic year. The registrar's office enters the course into the computer when the preregistration form has been signed by the department head signifying departmental approval. An applicant must have departmental approval in order to preregister for internship credit.

OBJECTIVES
AND GOALS

Figure 3-2 (continued)

4.   Between the preregistration period (in April) and registration (in August or February), the departmental internship supervisor contacts local organizations to ascertain the approximate number and types of placements available for the coming year. The period between preregistration and the student's actual involvement in the organization is a period for departmental planning and placement activities. Within the limits of potential placement number and types, the departmental internship supervisor places all applicants that the department has approved.

5.   During the term prior to the actual internship experience, the departmental internship supervisor establishes the placements between students and local organizations, and negotiates a contract of intern responsibilities. A copy of the intern's resume is sent to the organization with a copy of the responsibility contract.

6.   If the department has unused placements or new organizational contacts, a student may apply to the department for a late placement. Applications for late placements must be completed by October 1.

7.   The department reviews the late applications for placements between October 1 and the November preregistration change period. Departmental action is communicated in writing to the applicant by the department head. Approved applicants must change the student data sheet preregistration to include internships for January and spring with the department head's signature.

8.   Registration proceeds normally, and the intern reports to the organization at the designated time, after an orientation meeting with the departmental internship supervisor. The orientation meeting covers expected levels of performance, professional demeanor, dress, courtesy for necessary absences, etc.

9.   The departmental internship supervisor maintains contact with the intern and the organization supervisor during the internship period.

10. The departmental internship supervisor, the intern, and the organization supervisor complete designated assessment instruments. The departmental supervisor submits the internship grade to the registrar's office in accord with normal institutional reporting procedures.

Eligibility Requirements
Participation in an internship is a special privilege for students. To ensure that the experience is maximally beneficial to both the intern and the sponsoring organization, the following eligibility criteria have been adopted:

1.   The applicant must be classified as a senior at the time of the internship. Exceptions to this criterion must be carefully reviewed by the department, although it is understood that biology and chemistry premedical students may be granted the internship privilege prior to the senior year.

2.   All applicants must meet all requirements of the respective departments and have been accepted through the departmental application procedure.

(continued)

CHAPTER 3

Figure 3-2 (continued)

3.   Internships are generally available only in the student's major.

4.   The intern may earn up to, but no more than, six hours toward meeting minimum major hours. The internship may be repeated, not to exceed six hours per major.

5.   Registration and bill payment remain the student's responsibility.

6.   No intern may serve in an internship placement prior to departmental approval and completion of course registration.

7.   Placements are ordinarily established in the local community to ensure ongoing training of personnel at cooperating organizations and to facilitate adequate supervision by faculty. To avoid conflict of interest, students are not permitted to complete internships in businesses owned by the intern's family or to be supervised by family members.

8.   Teacher-education field teaching experiences are not considered internships; therefore they are not subject to the policies and procedures outlined in this document.

Internship Responsibilities
As a structured educational experience, the internship relies upon cooperation and coordination between the supervising department, the cooperating organization, and the intern. Each has special responsibilities in the internship process.

The College Department
1.   The department develops and implements admission requirements for the internship appropriate to its own curriculum.

2.   The department designates a faculty member to be responsible for internship placements and supervision (i.e., a departmental internship supervisor).

3.   The departmental internship supervisor negotiates intern responsibilities in a contract letter to the cooperating organization prior to placement.

4.   The department head files a list of all internship placements (cooperating organization and the student intern placed there) with the associate dean of instruction no later than the end of the first week of the term in which students are enrolled in internships.

5.   The department develops a supervisory policy to engage the faculty supervisor in the internship process and provide consistent guidance to the intern. Faculty supervision includes on-site visits in the initiation and evaluation stages of the internship, more often if possible.

6.   The department's supervising faculty member develops evaluation criteria and takes major responsibility for determination of the student's grade.

OBJECTIVES
AND GOALS

Figure 3-2 (continued)

7.   Should conditions warrant a change of responsibilities, a placement relocation, or withdrawal of the intern from a placement, the department develops and implements guidelines for such contingencies.

The Cooperating Organization

1.   The organization, in cooperation with the college department and the student, develops a written plan of activity suitable to its resources and the goals of the individual student to be placed therein. The plan clearly articulates the duties and responsibilities of the intern to the intern and supervising faculty.

2.   The organization designates an appropriate person to take primary responsibility for supervision of the intern.

3.   The organization provides appropriate guidance to the intern while actively engaged in the organization and provides assessments as agreed upon at the time of placement.

4.   The organization determines from its own policies the status of the intern and the rights and responsibilities of such a position. These are communicated to the department and the intern.

The Intern

1.   The intern contacts the department before March 1 for an internship in the following summer, fall, or spring.

2.   The intern meets all departmental requirements for application in a timely manner, including the initial application and final paper.

3.   The intern communicates regularly with the supervising faculty so that progress and/or difficulties may be confronted in a professional and timely manner.

4.   The intern dresses in accord with the professional expectations of the organization. The intern meets the time and professional courtesy expectations of the organization, including being punctual, being attentive, and calling the organizational supervisor when illness, etc. necessitates an absence.

5.   The intern takes the responsibility to represent the college and the department in a professional manner and be responsible to know and to practice the highest ethical standards appropriate to the college and to the professional setting in which he or she is serving.

6.   The intern completes all requirements of the department and the organization to the best of his or her ability.

7.   The intern is responsible for transportation to and from the internship placement.

(continued)

CHAPTER 3

Figure 3-2 (continued)

Performance Expectations

The expectations of performance that follow apply to most internship placements. Four key dimensions of behavior and demeanor are emphasized: personal habits, task performance, attitudes, and relationships. The intern is expected to monitor and conform to these expectations during the internship experience.

1. Personal Work Habits and Presentation of Self

The intern
> is punctual and dependable
> is self-reliant
> dresses neatly and appropriately
> has a pleasant, positive demeanor
> is attentive to others.

2. Skills in Task Performance

The intern
> completes assigned tasks
> attends to details
> manages time and energy well
> meets deadlines
> understands and follows directions
> seeks guidance when necessary
> demonstrates needed skills.

3. Attitudes

The intern
> demonstrates an active desire to learn from and contribute to the organization
> is open-minded and does not rush to judgment
> accepts and makes positive use of criticism
> understands and accepts the necessity of dull and repetitive tasks
> is inquisitive
> respects others' different skills and life orientations
> recognizes and accepts personal limitations
> is willing to accept new challenges
> maintains professional confidentiality
> understands the differences and strikes a balance between roles of employee and intern and
>> between the organization's goals and his or her own
> is cooperative, flexible, and adaptable

OBJECTIVES
AND GOALS

Figure 3-2 (continued)

demonstrates the ability to set, refine, and fulfill personal goals within those of the organization
shows openness to self-evaluation
seeks out resources within the organization and its affiliates.

4. Skills in Human Relations

The intern
adjusts to new circumstances, expectations, and people
develops alternative ways to respond when prior expectations are not met
questions and explores without putting others on the defensive
is sensitive to the needs and feelings of others
listens to others
copes well with unexpected problems
demonstrates tact
is appropriately assertive of personal views and concerns
tolerates ambiguity.

Finally, while most syllabi set out generic objectives for internship activity, some give a more focused view, like that published by the American Institute for Paralegal Studies, Inc. On the following page, Figure 3-3 provides the prospective intern with a true and clear understanding of the course and its policies. An intern can expect to do the following:

- apply ideas and concepts
- acquire new knowledge through experience
- analyze legal problems and situations
- observe various legal functions
- develop specific skills
- discover career options
- contribute to the legal field.

CHAPTER 3

Figure 3-3[3]

Course and Policies of Internship

1. The student will integrate the theoretical concepts and knowledge learned in the classroom with real-world employment situations (including law firms, corporations, and government agencies) under the direct supervision of a practicing attorney, paralegal or legal assistant, law librarian, or legal administrator.

2. The student will state the knowledge and skills he or she expects to acquire during the internship experience and will evaluate progress in attaining these objectives. (Refer to "Internship Authorization Form" and "Final Report.")

3. The student will work in a position where he or she performs the functions normally expected of a legal assistant or of an approved law-related position.

4. The student will gain experience working within the legal system and will gain confidence in his or her abilities as a legal assistant.

5. The student will have the opportunity to identify, develop, and create solutions to work-related problems.

6. The student will gain practical on-the-job experience in a professional legal setting.

7. The student will have the opportunity to observe the daily functioning of a law office and its interpersonal relationships.

8. The student will develop legal skills that are most effectively mastered in a legal setting.

9. The student will have the opportunity to explore a new career field.

10. The student's interest in academic classwork will be enhanced by increasing the student's ability to relate concepts to problems encountered during the internship.

11. The student will gain work-related references and networking opportunities which will enhance his or her marketability as a legal professional.

12. The student will learn to encourage attorneys to delegate work and will educate the attorneys as to the skills legal assistants possess.

13. The student will have the opportunity to demonstrate to attorneys the economic and non-economic value of employing legal assistants.

14. Feedback on the internship experience will provide a valuable source of information to the Institute's administration regarding the appropriateness and the effectiveness of the Institute's curriculum.

OBJECTIVES
AND GOALS

Internship Job
Description

After reviewing the previous pages, you can catalog the many personal, intellectual, and professional goals to be mastered and sought during the internship experience.

Another path to determining your internship goals and objectives is to address the responsibilities you will have. What exactly will you be doing? What is your job description? What types of functions, tasks, and responsibilities will you be assigned?

One of the most significant attractions of paralegalism is its eclectic nature; that is, its capacity to offer a diversity of tasks. A wise intern asks for a job description, or better yet, politely insists on a list of duties and responsibilities before tackling the job. One can hardly have goals or objectives for any experience if one has no notion of what is forthcoming. So don't be afraid to ask, "*What am I going to do?*"

Most individual employers/sponsors, agencies, or other entities will have a job description on file. Your program may list all paralegal functions in a preliminary job description such as the one in Figure 3-4.

Figure 3–4[4]

Checklist of Internship Tasks

The Institute is very happy to introduce you to our internship program. The internship program enables our students to gain practical paralegal work experience and offers our sponsors both economic and non-economic benefits, including redistribution of work loads, introduction to new skills, etc.

PURPOSE
- To give the Institute's students on-the-job training and experience prior to seeking employment as a paralegal or prior to changing positions within the legal services industry.

AIMS
- To allow students to participate in a work/study program in conjunction with their studies.

- To provide prospective employers with competent graduates who possess excellent academic background and quality work experience.

DURATION
- Attendance at internship orientation (two contact hours).

- Minimum of 90 hours performing legal assistant or directly related tasks.

CHAPTER 3

Figure 3-4 (continued)

OUTCOME
- Upon successful completion of the internship, a grade will be posted to the student's permanent record.

- The student will have gained practical paralegal work experience and an invaluable employment reference for future job searches.

Another approach to an effective internship is for the internship coordinator or other institutional authority to advise prospective supervisors of the tasks that interns can and should perform. See the checklist at Figure 3-5.

Figure 3-5[5]

Summary of Paralegal Tasks

A paralegal intern performs a multitude of tasks under the supervision of a sponsor. Creating a complete list of paralegal tasks is impossible; however, listed below are some of the broad areas where paralegals have proved to be very useful.

PREPARE BRIEFS AND MEMORANDA
- Check, Shepardize, and "bluebook" citations
- Proof documents
- Draft simple pleadings
- Draft fact sections of some briefs and memoranda
- Supervise mechanical production and distribution

PRODUCE AND ORGANIZE DOCUMENTS
- Assist in organizing and conducting file searches
- Digest, abstract, and index documents
- Develop a retrieval system
- Draft factual memoranda based on data contained in documents

48

OBJECTIVES AND GOALS

Figure 3-5 (continued)

PREPARE DEPOSITIONS
- Digest and index deposition transcripts
- Prepare materials to brief witnesses before deposition hearings
- Assist in briefing witnesses

PREPARE INTERROGATORIES/ANSWERS
- Organize and analyze answers to interrogatories
- Draft simple interrogatories and answers
- Assemble factual data used in preparing and answering interrogatories

PREPARE FOR TRIALS AND HEARINGS
- Gather and organize factual material for trials
- Develop charts, graphs, and other visual aids
- Take notes and handle exhibits at trials
- Assemble rebuttal evidence
- Digest and index transcripts

PLAN AND DEVELOP ESTATE DISTRIBUTION
- Collect data (e.g., birth dates, fair market value of assets, current assets)
- Write preliminary drafting of wills or trusts from sample forms
- Analyze investments

RESEARCH
- Obtain information from court records
- Research and analyze public records
- Prepare statistical and narrative reports
- Attend and report on legislative and administrative hearings
- Compile legislative histories

ADMINISTER AND MANAGE
- Maintain a master docket calendar
- Assist in administration of the law library
- Administer paralegal programs

Competencies of a Contract or Commercial Law Paralegal

Interns should also create a list of functions and tasks in the practice areas of expertise they seek. Several of these functions must be performed under the supervision of an attorney. Following is a series of these competencies, categorized by legal topic.

49

CHAPTER 3

- Identify a legally enforceable contract.
- Draft contracts that contain the requisite elements for enforceability.
- Recognize and explain those conditions that serve to terminate an offer or that constitute a counteroffer.
- Recognize the means and methods by which an offer may be revoked.
- Draft correspondence and other documents highlighting the precise nature of an offer or acceptance and outlining the specificity of consideration.
- Recognize the distinction between a bilateral and unilateral contract.
- Transmit a proper notice of acceptance.
- Determine whether consideration is legally adequate.
- Make a chart, list, or graph outlining contracts that require a writing under the Statute of Frauds.
- Pinpoint contracts that do not require a writing.
- Make judgments concerning the legal competency of individuals to enter into contracts, particularly in the consumer finance environment.
- Recognize contractual activities that will be void for public policy and are inherently illegal.
- Distinguish normal sales ability from techniques of fraud, misrepresentation, and duress.
- Make recommendations regarding the overall enforceability of a contract defense.
- Draft affirmative defense clauses in a contract between parties.
- List and specify rights in third-party beneficiaries including creditors, donees, and subcontractors.
- Draft and design an assignment of rights agreement.
- Identify those services, tasks, or duties that can be delegated.
- Draft and design a delegation of duties contract.
- Draft conditional clauses and contingencies.
- Recognize conduct that can be viewed as a present, actual and/or anticipatory breach of performance.
- Make qualitative judgments regarding the major or minor nature of a breach.
- Make recommendations on a legal rationale or excuse from contract performance including a failure of conditions, waiver, and estoppel.
- Identify, recognize, and explain the conditions that result in a discharge of obligations due to factual and legal impossibility.
- Define standardized, consequential, and liquidated damages and explain the circumstances under which each applies.
- Define and explain compensatory, punitive, and nominal damages.
- Calculate damage claims.
- Calculate a liquidated damage claim.
- Draft notice, correspondence, and other documentation putting a defendant on notice of his or her breach of contract.
- Draft documents and other memoranda highlighting the inability to meet or perform an existing condition for contractual contingency.

OBJECTIVES
AND GOALS

- Recognize an Article 2 sale of goods.
- Cite when a sale of goods under Article 2 must be perfected under Article 9.
- Make recommendations on the contract's unconscionability in a contract's provisions.
- Draft and design provisions that provide for implied warranty and merchantability and warranty of fitness for a particular purpose.
- Make recommendations on specific remedies that buyers and sellers can take under a contract or sale of goods under UCC's Article 2.
- Evaluate fact patterns in order to give alternative remedies to both buyers and sellers in a typical commercial transaction.
- Recognize all forms of commercial paper.
- Present commercial paper for acceptance in payment.
- Acquire surety documents.
- Prepare and draft a bill of lading.
- Properly endorse negotiable instruments.
- Endorse and transfer a stock certificate and draft an assignment separate from certificate.
- Register bonds and stocks.
- Negotiate bearer bonds.
- Read and utilize the UCC or applicable state statutes.
- Define an Article 9 secured interest.
- Discern whether attachment of a secured interest has taken place.
- Perfect a security interest.
- Determine who has priority in a secured interest.
- Prepare correspondence necessary under federal and state regulations for consumer finance, including notices, Regulation Z, and other financing documents.
- File financing documents with the secretary of state, county, or other local officials as required under local rules and law.
- Finance a transaction using documents as collateral.
- Finance a transaction using inventory as collateral.
- Finance a motor vehicle.
- Finance equipment as a source of collateral.
- Determine which parties must file to perfect their interest.
- Determine where the parties must file to perfect their interest.
- Make recommendations on an outline of ownership priority in a secured interest.
- Perfect the security interest in the following ways:
  - possession of the collateral
  - a financing statement in a designated public office
  - automatic perfection upon the attachment of the security interest
  - temporary perfection for a limited period of time.

CHAPTER 3

Competencies of a Bankruptcy Law Paralegal

- Provide lists of documents required for filing preparation, i.e., tax returns, life insurance policies, list of liabilities, and financial statements.
- Collect personal financial information and prepare list of assets.
- Maintain a tickler and calendar system, including status sheet.
- Survey court records of lawsuits and judgments against the debtor.
- Obtain UCC and real property searches, as well as appraisals.
- File a wage-earner plan schedule and fee with a bankruptcy court.
- Check creditor documentation to ensure proper perfection.
- Attend court hearings with attorney and client.
- Conduct an initial interview to obtain information for filing a petition and schedules, etc.
- Familiarize a client with general procedures at hearings, meetings and, motions.
- Analyze and summarize factual information.
- Meet with a client to review and sign schedules.
- Draft and file a bankruptcy petition and schedules.
- Draft and file a proof of claim for bankruptcy.
- Process letters to creditors with a copy of order for relief.
- Prepare preliminary drafts of questions for the first creditor meeting.
- Attend the first meeting of creditors.
- Collect data for a creditor's proof of claim in bankruptcy.
- Prepare a plan of reorganization and disclosure statements.
- Draft, serve, and file Chapter 11 debtor's monthly financial statements.
- Help prepare pleadings for adversary proceedings.
- Compile initial schedules for a bankrupt wage-earner plan.
- Write proof of claim of a wage-earner plan.
- Prepare preliminary drafts of questions for various hearings.
- Prepare legal, financial, and statistical research.
- Draft reaffirmation agreements.
- Contact creditors and complete related forms.
- Draft various motions, including those for avoidance of liens.
- Handle routine telephone calls and correspondence.
- Draft and file attorney's fee applications with the bankruptcy court.[6]
- Attend court hearings to ease flow of documents and information.
- Draft, serve, and file complaints in adversary proceedings.
- Attend a Section 341 (a) meeting.
- Attend a Chapter 13 Plan confirmation hearing.
- Obtain a list of creditors.

Competencies of an Estates and Trusts Paralegal

- List all tasks, duties, and obligations of a paralegal in an estate planning practice.
- Chart and diagram the intestate succession laws of the paralegal's jurisdiction.
- Calculate property distribution under an intestate succession statute.
- Draft and design an estate planning interview form and checklist.

OBJECTIVES AND GOALS

- Make a list, diagram, or chart of the formal requirements for drafting wills that covers capacity, execution, and attestation requirements and essential clauses.
- Draft and design specific will clauses and provisions.
- Draft and design residuary estate clauses.
- Draft and design a testamentary trust within a will.
- Draft and design checklists, interview documents, and other materials that will help in the collection of information for will construction.
- Designate parties as either donor or donee, settlor or beneficiary.
- Draft and design a trust for asset or financial management purposes.
- Draft or design a trust for charitable purposes.
- Draft or design a trust for minimization of tax liability.
- Draft or design a general trust that includes provisions for the marital deduction, alternative distribution techniques, and powers of appointment.
- Draft and design forms, checklists, and other exhibits necessary for information gathering in the trust process.
- Understand the functions of trustees and executors.
- Be familiar with the various services offered by the trust departments of local financial institutions in the paralegal's jurisdiction.
- Draft clauses on revocability in a trust document.
- Understand the legal effect of a Totten trust.
- Provide information to clients regarding the implications of the Tax Reform Act of 1986.
- Draft the provision of a trust that outlines the powers, duties, and obligations of a trustee.
- Draft documents signifying the resignation of a trustee.
- Devise checklists, forms, and other materials that chart, track, and provide a history of estate planning assets and important individuals.
- Design personal and family information sheets.
- Locate all necessary legal documents to begin the administration of an estate, including trusts, gift documents, wills, certificates, and titles.
- Become skilled in the search of records at governmental offices such as the Registrar of Wills, the Surrogate or Orphan Court, the Office of Vital Statistics, Veteran's Administration, and the Social Security Administration.
- Create a chart, graph, or diagram listing all government agencies that deal with the administration of estates, along with the agencies' phone numbers and addresses.
- Collect information on the business interests of the estate, including assets owned by corporations, partnerships, or sole proprietorships.
- Collect all forms and documents necessary for initial estate filing.
- Acquire statutory or legislative codes on estate administration.
- Make a list, chart, or diagram of all responsible local court personnel who handle the administration of estates.
- Draft, under the supervision of an attorney, a petition to identify heirs.

CHAPTER 3

- Acquire all forms and documents necessary for either formal or informal, supervised or independent probate proceedings.
- Prepare preliminary drafts of and file documents, such as a petition for a grant of letters testamentary or probate, or other pleadings necessary to effect a probate proceeding.
- Prepare a notice and/or order of Hearing of Appointment and Admission of Will to Probate.
- Prepare inventory of estate assets.
- Prepare an information sheet mailed to beneficiaries under the probate process.
- Prepare a notice to creditors.
- Calculate and determine a spouse's elective right under the statutory code of the paralegal's jurisdiction.
- Calculate and assess multiple problems under a spouse's right of election.
- Pay taxes from an estate administration fund.
- Handle specific claims for which the estate is liable.
- Perform a final accounting on an estate.
- Calculate attorney and/or executor's fees based on agreed upon formulas.
- Perform a closing procedure on an estate.
- Collect tax forms and documents for estate and gift calculation.
- Calculate unified credits on an estate tax return.
- Identify those assets that would be construed as transfers made in contemplation of death.
- Employ and use specific transitional rules in the determination of a gross estate.
- Perform multiple methods of valuation of an estate.
- Complete an estate and gift tax return.
- Compute unified credits, annual exclusions, deductions, and exemptions under the estate and gift tax rules and principles.
- Identify all types of wills recognized by the laws of the paralegal's jurisdiction.
- Identify all parties named in a will by designation, such as testator, testatrix, executor, executrix, guardian, trustee, etc.
- Develop effective docket procedures to ensure timely filing of all probate and tax documents.
- Develop effective procedures for making final distribution of assets.

Competencies of an Investigative Paralegal

- Participate in the initial phases of case evaluation to determine whether further investigation is necessary.
- Develop the requisite skills of objectivity, logic, and perseverance in the investigative process.
- Develop good human relations skills in dealing with clients, witnesses, sources, etc.
- Be able to differentiate the many types of witnesses in an investigative process.
- Locate missing or unknown witnesses.
- Draft and maintain a listing of expert organizations.

OBJECTIVES AND GOALS

- Contact medical and specialty expert organizations for assistance in evaluating evidence.
- Draft correspondence and questionnaires to be sent to witnesses for the attorney's approval.
- Draft interrogatories and direct or cross-examination inquiries for expert witness testimony for the attorney's review.
- Interview, take the depositions, and coach witnesses.
- Develop a solid and ongoing relationship with contacts, both public and private.
- Develop a relationship with private companies who can assist in locating missing witnesses.
- Be aware of and know how to use the many sources of information available in the investigative process.
- Become familiar with and be able to gain access to the investigative documentation and methods employed by police departments.
- Draft checklists and logs for use in collecting physical evidence.
- Develop and maintain a comprehensive investigative kit for the collection and preservation of evidence.
- Become familiar with and practice the various methods of preserving and transmitting evidence.
- Reconstruct events based upon the facts at hand.
- Photograph or graphically recreate an accident scene.
- Draft correspondence to medical facilities or personnel necessary to acquire medical records.
- Draft correspondence to state and federal governmental entities to acquire accident date.
- Draft a comprehensive accident scene investigation report.
- Sort, categorize, and maintain the physical evidence, correspondence, statements, and other information collected in the investigative process.

Competencies of a Criminal Law Paralegal

- Summarize and annotate lower court transcripts for appeal.
- Analyze bank records and preparation of check spreads.
- Review corporate records, including minutes and financial data.
- Review and analyze tax records and supporting documentation.
- Log exhibits offered and admitted.
- Log objections sustained and overruled.
- Monitor jury's reactions during trial.
- Help with preparation of opening and closing arguments.
- Prepare outline of prosecution and defense cases.
- Coordinate specific documents with a witness during testimony.
- Verify that all depositions have been filed.
- Help in planning and strategy.
- Take notes and monitor related hearings and trials.
- Help in preparing witnesses for testimony in trial or deposition.
- Investigate background information on potential jurors.

CHAPTER 3

- Draft jury instructions.
- Help with analysis of *voir dire*.
- Prepare complete notes of witness testimony.
- Help with interviewing a jury following the verdict.
- Attend and help at trial.
- Attend client and attorney meetings regarding presentence reports.
- Prepare sentencing information and work with probation officers.
- Research the law regarding appealable issues.
- Draft assignments of error and arguments.

Competencies of a Personal Injury and Tort Law Paralegal

- Understand the various forms of tortious conduct.
- Distinguish between tortious and criminal conduct and the possibility of simultaneous occurrence.
- Distinguish between intentional and negligent tortious conduct, and the possibility of simultaneous occurrence.
- Gain understanding of the nature of strict liability.
- Classify claimant as trespasser, licensee, or invitee.
- Draft forms, checklists, and logs for use in assessing the tort claim.
- Participate in the initial interview of clients to assess the merits of the claim.
- Apply the concepts of foreseeability, duty owed, and reasonable person to the facts of the case.
- Determine the existence of multiple defendants in a claim.
- Determine the existence or nonexistence of the client's contributory or comparative negligence in the claim.
- Collect and assemble evidence of damages, physical and economic.
- Calculate damages based upon injuries sustained.
- Locate and interview witnesses.
- Locate technical experts to assist in case evaluation/reconstruction.
- Perform legal research.
- Research and review insurance policy limits, underinsured and uninsured benefits.
- Draft correspondence to product manufacturers, designers, and retailers.
- Create and maintain a tickler/calendaring system to insure the integrity of a claim.
- Draft demand letters in personal injury, medical malpractice, and product liability cases.
- Draft follow-up correspondence regarding demand letter status.
- Draft pleadings appropriate to the tortious conduct claimed.
- Draft interrogatories, answers, defenses, and counter or cross-claims.
- Become knowledgeable of the various forms of affirmative defenses.
- Obtain medical authorizations.
- Determine what medical records are needed and request same.
- Arrange for independent medical exams.
- Draft submissions to the medical review panel board.
- Schedule appointments with clients, attorneys, adjusters, and experts.

OBJECTIVES AND GOALS

- Attend meetings of attorneys and doctors; prepare memoranda.
- Handle routine correspondence, such as updating clients.
- Review all case files on a periodic basis and follow up on status.
- Review medical and forensic publications.
- Conduct client interviews.
- Review medical records and reports.
- Extract data from medical reports and annotate them.
- Ascertain amounts and categories of damages for settlement.
- Obtain medical expert opinions.
- Prepare submissions to various funds or to the Department of Insurance.
- Prepare pleadings required to open estates in wrongful death cases.
- Research and review general areas of the law in a case.
- Research and review medical topics.
- Design and prepare graphs, transparencies, charts, and trial aids.[7]

Competencies of a Family Law Paralegal

- Attend the initial interview with an attorney and client.
- Collect background information on a client.
- Complete a domestic relations questionnaire form.
- Do legal research.
- Draft a notice to produce.
- Serve a notice on opposing counsel.
- Arrange for a service of documents.
- Conduct follow-up filing petitions and checking service.
- Conduct timely briefings of a client concerning the status of the case.
- Set trial dates and prepare necessary notification to all parties.
- Help a client in preparation of monthly income and expense sheet.
- Arrange for an appraisal of real property and personal property.
- Schedule expert witness interviews and confirm the witnesses' availability for trial.
- Close cases and clean up the file.
- Research tax aspects of child support/maintenance.
- Determine protection available in domestic violence incidents.
- Draft a petition for name change.
- Prepare forms necessary to transfer property.
- Inform or notify insurance companies that may be affected by the claim.
- Determine if property has been delivered to the rightful owner.
- Keep track of monetary property settlement payment dates.
- File the legal documents to enforce judgments.
- Identify nonlegal problems that can be referred to other entities.
- Draft a petition for dissolution or response.
- Draft temporary motions, affidavits, and orders.
- Draft a property settlement agreement.
- Determine child and/or spousal support needs.
- Draft a decree of dissolution, accompanying motions, and affidavits.

CHAPTER 3

- Draft a motion and an affidavit for modification.
- Communicate with any opposing counsel or client.
- Maintain contact; handle calls when legal advice is not needed.
- Obtain and organize information for discovery.
- Draft proposed stipulations.
- Confer with a client before court on issues relevant to a hearing.
- Draft a petition for consent for and decree of adoption.
- Draft post-decree pleadings as necessary.
- Prepare court documents, unusual petitions, and accountings.
- Develop and maintain manual or computerized accounting procedures.
- Develop and maintain manual or computerized client database.
- Develop and maintain tax, probate, and other manuals.[8]

Competencies of a Real Estate Paralegal

- Draft closing documents, including...
    - deed of conveyance
    - bill of sale
    - affidavit of title
    - American Land Title Association (ALTA) statement
    - release
    - collateral assignment documents
    - lease
    - transfer declaration
    - assignment
    - closing/settlement statement
    - lien waiver
    - rent schedule
    - lease schedule.
- Set up land trusts and draft land trust documents, including...
    - trust agreement
    - direction to convey
    - letter of direction
    - assignment of beneficial interest
    - deed in trust
    - trustee's deed
    - certified resolution.
- Order title commitment and abstract searches.
- Review exceptions to title.
- Prepare or obtain necessary documents to correct or clear title and obtain certain endorsements.
- Order and review plat of survey.
- Review leases, prepare tenant estoppel letters, and coordinate the execution.
- Contact the holder of an existing loan to arrange for payoff or to obtain lender's estoppel letter.
- Order and review utility letters, soil tests, environmental surveys, zoning compliance letters, building permits, and building code violation printout.

58

OBJECTIVES
AND GOALS

- Coordinate the details of closings with local counsel, real estate brokers, clients, title company, and opposing counsel.
- Review a management agreement and service contract and prepare compilations.
- Attend a property inspection.
- Prepare a checklist of documents and items to be obtained or accomplished at closing.
- Attend and assist the attorney at closing.
- Coordinate post-closing matters, including recording documents, wiring funds, obtaining cancellation documents, issuance of owner's and loan policies, organizing and indexing files, and overseeing preparation of closing document binders.
- Order and review an estimate of redemption for real estate taxes.
- Record mortgage, deed, assignment release, and other documents.
- Order duplicate tax receipts and assemble same.
- Prepare Forms 1099A, 1099S, and 1096 for qualifying transactions.
- Draft and review permits.
- Draft, review, and plot legal descriptions.
- Redline changes in documents upon revision.
- Draft and arrange for filing of Uniform Commercial Code (UCC) [financing statements, amendments, extensions or terminations].
- Analyze and digest leases, assignments, extensions, and amendments not of record.
- Arrange for payoff of notes and release of mortgages and trust deeds.
- Obtain closing figures from closing party and determine the necessary closing amount.
- Notarize documents at closing, if qualified.
- Assist a client in obtaining liability insurance.
- Order UCC, Totten, judgment, and tax lien searches.
- Monitor and obtain a release of bulk sales stop order.
- Order certified copies of certain real estate and partnership documents.
- Prepare and file assumed name application.
- Know and use certain county, city, and municipal offices regarding recordings, conveyances, land use planning, zoning, annexation, real estate tax matters, and building code violations.
- Maintain firm form files.
- Attend negotiations and discussions relating to the terms of the sale contract.
- Draft the sale contract, assignments thereof, and amendments thereto.
- Draft an exchange agreement and attend relevant negotiations.
- Draft a loan commitment and attend relevant negotiations.
- Draft an installment sale contract and attend relevant negotiations.
- Draft deed and money, money lenders, joint order, and construction escrows.
- Draft partnership agreements, amendments and certificates of partnership.

CHAPTER 3

- Draft additional closing documents, including loan agreements, notes, security agreements, mortgages, estoppel certificates, buy-sell agreements, indemnification agreements, participation agreements, subordination agreements, nondisturbance agreements, guaranties, opinions of counsel, option agreements, trade name registrations, easement agreements, restrictive covenants, and all other closing documents necessary for a transaction to close.
- Prepare a preliminary abstract of title and draft an opinion on the title and issue policy.
- Check for compliance with truth-in-lending requirements.
- Assist in resolving real estate tax problems, such as reassessment/valuation complaints and tax parcel divisions or consolidations.[9]

Competencies of a Civil Litigation Paralegal

- Arrange for an outside investigator.
- Handle computerized research for source materials.
- Conduct factual research.
- Conduct an initial client interview.
- Draft demand letters.
- Photograph accident scenes, evidence, and/or the parties.
- Locate, interview, and obtain statements of witnesses.
- Trace documents and physical evidence.
- Search records from private and public sources.
- Draft documents including complaints, answers, interrogatories, requests for production of documents, requests for examination, requests for admissions, affidavits, motions for extension of time, trial briefs, *voir dire* questions, jury instructions, etc.
- Review client files, gather and organize factual data.
- Prepare and serve subpoenas and subpoena duces tecum.
- Index/abstract documents.
- Review documents for responsiveness to production requests.
- Prepare statistical and economic information.
- Review and summarize medical and other records.
- Index and summarize depositions and deposition exhibits.
- Keep current with procedures of local, state, and federal courts.
- Organize witness files.
- Arrange for publication of legal notices.
- Maintain court calendar (docket) on tickler system.
- Arrange for extensions of time by telephone, letter, or motion.
- Meet with a client to prepare answers to interrogatories and obtain a client's documents to be produced: medical records, wage and wage loss information, tax statements, photographs, bills or expenses that were incurred because of the lawsuits, etc.
- Attend and organize document productions.
- Attend on-site and expert inspections.
- Prepare, organize, and supervise document control systems.
- Create database and procedures for computerized systems.

OBJECTIVES
AND GOALS

- Input information into database.
- Research facts for depositions.
- Draft outline and questions for depositions.
- Prepare witnesses for deposition.
- Schedule, attend, and take notes at depositions.
- Organize exhibits and request copies of a transcript.
- Follow up after a deposition for additional information.
- Segregate and record documents not to be produced and privileged materials, for attorney's review.
- Locate expert witnesses; interview and prepare written reports.
- Prepare statistical/factual memoranda.
- Prepare status reports on a case to be submitted to the client.
- Compile product history; obtain information about similar products, market surveys, and industrial statistics in product liability cases.
- Draft legal memoranda or briefs.
- Perform legal research, cite check, and Shepardize.
- Review and analyze a case continually for further discovery.
- Prepare and exchange names of witnesses and exhibit lists.
- Prepare trial notebooks and witness files.
- Prepare graphs, charts, etc.
- Arrange for a court reporter and computerized transcript.
- Prepare, mark, and index exhibits.
- Prepare outlines of anticipated testimony.
- Meet with witnesses, help in preparation of witness and client testimony, and coordinate attendance at the trial.
- Help in analysis of video and audio evidence at the trial.
- Draft pretrial statements, settlement calculations (including comparative analysis of potential settlement terms) and a settlement conference memo.
- Obtain the jury list and do biographical research on each juror.
- Draft a bill of costs.
- Draft a settlement documents, including releases, dismissals, and satisfaction.
- Maintain a list of exhibits offered, admitted, or objected to.
- Prepare digests, abstracts, indices and/or summaries of transcripts.
- Attend trial: take notes of testimony, and reaction of jurors, witnesses, and counsel; organize exhibits, documents, coordination of witnesses and experts.
- Help in jury selection: prepare *voir dire* questions, observe jurors' reactions and responses, and review and analyze jurors' questionnaires.
- Prepare draft of document list and testimony used to impeach opposition witnesses.
- Help in preparing witnesses.
- Gather documents and pertinent information with which to familiarize the witness with the issues and facts of the case.
- Draft notice of appeal.

CHAPTER 3

- Order hearing transcript; prepare recap or outline of transcripts.
- Set up timetable for filings.
- Help in preparation of record on appeal.

Course Evaluation Policy

As a prospective intern, you should anticipate how your performance will be evaluated. What means will be used to assess how well or even how poorly you did? How will you be evaluated and by whom? Will there be assignments of any kind, tests and reports? How will these requirements be calculated and weighed?

In the most generic sense, a prospective intern can see the internship within the demands of a published grading policy. Figure 3-6 illustrates a sound and simple grading policy that accomplishes two ends: first, it tells what is required: a sponsor evaluation, logs, and a final report; and second, it sets out the letter grading scale policy.

Figure 3-6[18]

Grading Policy

The following items will be used to determine the student's grade for the internship:

A. Sponsor's evaluation:
   Performance (50 percent)
B. Placement director's evaluation:
   Daily log (25 percent)
   Final report (25 percent)

The daily log and final report are graded based upon the student's thoroughness, organization, and thoughtfulness.

Grading Scale:
A numerical grade will be assigned. The numerical grade is converted into a letter grade as follows:

97 — 100	A+
94 — 96	A
90 — 93	A-
87 — 89	B+
84 — 86	B
80 — 83	B -
77 — 79	C+
74 — 76	C
70 — 73	C-
67 — 69	D+
64 — 66	D
60 — 63	D-
59 or below	F

OBJECTIVES
AND GOALS

A — Excellent performance.
B — Good performance.
   Performance demonstrates a good combination of personal and professional qualities.
C — Satisfactory performance.
   The student did what was expected but did not demonstrate superior initiative, adaptability, and professional performance.
D — Unsatisfactory performance.
   In some programs, a grade lower than C is unacceptable and the internship will have to be repeated.

In addition, this policy computes grades both numerically and alphabetically and puts students on notice of these quantitative measures.

When these quantitative measures are coupled with a series of student responsibilities, no intern will be unprepared or unable to determine clear objectives. See Figure 3-7 for an excellent list of student responsibilities.

Figure 3-7[11]

Student Responsibilities

1. In order to receive credit for this course, the student must attend the two-hour internship orientation class and must work a minimum of 90 hours in the internship itself. The hours worked must be spent learning the functions of a paralegal or actually performing paralegal or related functions.

2. The student is responsible for locating possible internship opportunities and arranging interviews with potential sponsors.

3. The student and the intern sponsor must complete the internship authorization form. The internship is subject to the placement director's approval.

4. The student will give one copy of the signed internship authorization form to the sponsor, send one copy to the placement department, and keep one copy for personal reference.

5. The student may begin working only after the intern receives written approval from the placement department.

6. The student must complete and return the mid-internship evaluation form.

(continued)

CHAPTER 3

Figure 3-7 (continued)

7. The student must keep a daily log of activities, indicating the amount of time spent performing the various paralegal tasks and a description of the tasks. The daily log must be submitted to the placement director at the end of the internship. Please refer to the "Guidelines for Internship Log" (p. 69) and "Internship Daily Log" (p. 71).

8. The student must complete a final report that demonstrates the application of legal skills in a job-related setting. Please refer to "Final Report Guidelines" below.

9. The student is responsible for notifying the placement department of any problems that may occur while working with the internship sponsor.

10. All students must complete the internship within the institute's established period of completion (within four semesters of the student's entry into the paralegal program). For example, a student who starts the paralegal program in September 1995 must complete the internship requirements no later than August 1997.

Finally, the majority of internship programs require a written report upon internship completion. Prospective interns know what constitutes an acceptable report before their internship begins. Detailed instructions and guidelines, as in Figure 3-8, go a long way toward preparing the intern for the experiences to come.

Figure 3-8[12]

Guidelines for a Final Report

The purpose of the Final Report is to review, describe, evaluate, and discuss the detailed process and accomplishments gained from the internship experience. It is a report that assesses the comprehensive benefits gained by the intern as well as by the internship sponsor. The report will be assigned a letter grade based on neatness, logical thought processes, correct grammatical usage, as well as cognitive ideas and concepts.

After completing the 90 hours of internship work experience, the student must submit the Final Report to the placement department to summarize the internship experience.

The paper should be no more than five typed pages in length.

OBJECTIVES AND GOALS

Figure 3-8 (continued)

The report should include:

1. Cover page showing student's name, address, telephone number; internship sponsor's name, firm, address, telephone number; dates of the internship.

2. Description of tasks performed and number of hours devoted to each task. State skills used and identify where the skills were acquired (names, sponsor's support staff, etc.).

3. Description of the law firm or business practice, including descriptions of the personnel and the student's relationship to other personnel in the office, including the supervising attorney. Include specific illustrations and examples. An organizational chart can be included.

4. Evaluation of the benefit derived from the assignments in terms of the intern's personal goals. Compare the knowledge and skills actually gained with the knowledge and skills that had been expected. Describe personal performance in each task category, referencing specific work produced and forms used. Describe any problems that arose while performing assigned tasks.

5. Description of paralegal billing procedures and minimum billing expectations/requirements.

6. Discussion of the benefits provided to the internship sponsor as a result of the internship program. Also describe how these benefits might relate to future employment opportunities.

7. Evaluation and summary of the internship experience including general opinions, observations, complaints, etc. Also address the impact of the internship on career orientation, skills acquisition, human relations, and job improvement.

8. Assessment of how the Institute's program prepared the student for the experience and how it might offer better preparation.

9. Inclusion of, as necessary, any insights, comments, and/or recommendations that have occurred in the internship but have not been addressed in prior sections.

Attachments to the Final Report

1. With permission of the sponsor, you may attach sample work completed. Delete client names and numbers to respect confidentiality. Copies of documents, forms, letters, pleadings, memoranda, research projects, and other work products developed or used would be appropriate. All documents may be maintained in an internship portfolio.

2. Daily Log.

(continued)

CHAPTER 3

Figure 3-8 (continued)

Due Date

1. The Final Report is due three weeks after completing the 90 hours of on-site work.

2. All requirements for the internship must be completed within the Institute's period of completion. Please refer to the Institute's official student catalog for the period of completion policy.

Tracking the Internship Experience

Few courses in the academic setting have the impact of an internship. During internships, theoretical knowledge is tested, ivory tower principles are analyzed, and interns discover their suitability for the career they have chosen. Compared to the classroom, the internship is an unpredictable experience, not constrained by classroom walls. Dramatic change can occur, both personal and professional, during the intern's tenure. Minimal changes probably imply a poor, unrewarding experience.

Mike Milstein's work on internship programs insightfully creates differentiated stages to measure change. See Figure 3-9 for a modification of his plan.

OBJECTIVES AND GOALS

Figure 3-9

Assessment of the Internship Experience

Evaluation Topics	Admission to Intern Programs	Early Clinical Experiences	Midpoint Feedback	Closing Stages of Program	Post-Program
Potential as a paralegal					
Career direction as a paralegal					
Professional growth needs as a paralegal					
Internship activities					
Mindset: To paralegal career					
Resource Use: People and materials					
Networking					
Readiness to enter job market					

CHAPTER 3

In Milstein's model, the topics to be evaluated can be assessed at five points in time:

admission to intern programs
early clinical experiences
midpoint feedback
closing stages of program
post-program.

Strategies that realistically measure the internship experience follow.

The Log or Diary

A log or diary traditionally means a written commentary on actual experiences. In the internship setting, logs or diaries are a written evaluation of what is happening to you. Logs can take the form of notes, an essay, or a written memorandum to your internship advisor. Placing your thoughts on paper will force you to think through the experience and will give you a historical perspective over the course of the internship.[14]

Because memories are unreliable, the log or diary can retrace the steps the intern took throughout the internship and trap perceptions according to a specific task or action. Logs and diaries serve a twofold purpose: first, a functional one — cataloging the performed tasks and corresponding responsibilities, and second, measuring and qualifying the intern's reaction to both actions and setting.

Logs and diaries take various forms and measure reactions in either broad or specific terms. A well-designed log poses questions for interns to ponder. It is a good policy for the educational institution or faculty member to provide instructions or guidelines on the use and completion of logs. Two guidelines are provided at Figure 3-10 and Figure 3-11. Both require the intern to do the following:

make daily notations
list activities
focus on new skills
list likes and dislikes
give comments.

OBJECTIVES
AND GOALS

Figure 3-10[15]

Guidelines for Internship Log

The student must maintain a daily log, written in ink or typed. The log resembles a time sheet commonly used by law offices for billable hours. The log should indicate the date, the client (do not use the real client's name), the client number, the matter number, the activity work code (which reflects the type of work accomplished), the amount of time spent on each task, as well as any additional comments necessary to define the task. A separate log sheet should be used for each day of the internship. The overall content will be judged on neatness, detail, and the extent the student has provided a complete analysis and thoughtful introspection in addition to simply logging internship hours.

The completed log will be submitted to the placement director at the end of the internship and must include the following information:

1. The intern and sponsor's names and a date.

2. The client name or topic. Please respect the confidentiality of the law firm.

3. Client numbers, matter numbers and activity work codes can be specific to each law office.

   Client number: Used to identify the client in the filing/billing system.

   Matter number: Identifies the specific client file, i.e., clients can have more than one file.

   Activity work code: Refers to a specific work task completed. **For confidentiality purposes, please do not use the exact client numbers used by the organization for which you are interning.** In addition, please use the enclosed "timekeeping codes" when completing the activity work code portion of the daily log. If the law firm for which you are interning uses a different set of "timekeeping codes" you may use those; however, you must provide a copy of those codes with your daily log.

4. The time spent performing the work in 15-minute increments (or in the sponsor's standard billing increments).

5. Additional comments in order to clearly define the work task.

6. New tasks, techniques, principles, forms, or documents encountered as part of the daily assigned responsibilities.

7. Other comments and observations regarding the work environment and specific tasks, including any problems encountered and method of resolving problems.

8. Total time complete for the day.

9. The sponsor's initials at the bottom of each completed log sheet (one log sheet per day).

CHAPTER 3

Figure 3-11 characterizes services rendered or activities engaged in by an assigned code. To illustrate, if the paralegal is asked to research a particular legal question or a statute number of proposed legislation, the activity correlates with a suggested code number (See Figure 3-12).

Any code system can work according to specific time lines as shown in the daily log format at Figure 3-11. Its layout computes the activity work code as well as time intervals. In the majority of internship programs, time is equated with credit hours awarded. The standard formula based on a credit system is

1 credit hour	=	45 hours
2 credit hours	=	90 hours
3 credit hours	=	135 hours

Any log document that calculates time must evidence time expended and note time remaining.

Use the facts below to prepare a daily log:

- 9:00-9:30 A.M. — conference with supervisor regarding the day's activities

- 9:30-10:15 A.M. — prepared six memos for supervisor, as follows:

to Mary Smith _____	Client # 67
for John Jones _____	Client # 12
for Andrew Brown _____	Client # 30
to Darla Barton _____	Client # 6
for Theresa Collins_____	Client # 89
to Theresa Collins _____	Client # 89

- 10:15-11:00 A.M. — reviewed case material (Client # 55) for upcoming interview

- 11:00-12:00 P.M. — met with Client # 55 for interview

- 12:00-12:30 P.M. — lunch

- 12:30-2:45 P.M. — researched various statutes on bankruptcy law for case of Client # 67

- 2:45-4:00 P.M. — attended hearing of Client # 94 with supervisor

- 4:00-5:00 P.M. — reviewed testimony from hearing of Client # 94

**OBJECTIVES
AND GOALS**

Figure 3-11[16]

Daily Log Sample

Daily Time Record For_____   Date_____
                                                     Page_____

Internship Sponsor _____

Use 15-minute Intervals:
15 minutes = .25 hour /30 minutes = .50 hour /45 minutes = .75 hour /60 minutes = 1.00 hour

Client/Matter

    (Respect client confidentiality. Create fictitious names to represent a client's case.)
     • See Time Keeping Codes for Code Description

Client	Client #	Matter #	Activity Work Code #	Time	Comments
Firm Administration	9999	1	101	1.0	meeting with atty. reviews
American Corporation	12345	89-0029	110	2.25	ass't w/ prep of memo

List new tasks, techniques, principles, statutes, and forms/documents experienced in the day's responsibilities.

_____

_____

_____

(continued)

CHAPTER 3

Figure 3-11 (continued)

Comment on observations and feelings regarding the work environment and specific tasks, including problems encountered and resolutions accomplished.

Total Time for the day _____   Sponsor's Initials _____

Figure 3-12[17]

Daily Log Codes

Activities

100	In-person conference participation with client
101	In-person conference with supervisor
102	Miscellaneous in-person conference
103	Telephone conference with client
104	Telephone conference with supervisor
105	Miscellaneous telephone conference
106	Review/receipt of correspondence regarding client case
107	Correspondence to client
108	Correspondence for client
109	Correspondence to other legal counsel
110	Participated in preparation of memoranda
111	Conducted/assisted in legal research
112	Conducted/assisted factual investigations
113	Reviewed/examined records
114	Reviewed pleadings, briefs, and/or memoranda
115	Reviewed/participated in automated systems, such as document assembly, time/billing, and docket/calender
116	Assisted filing procedure with the court system
117	Observed trial, deposition, etc.
118	Updated and/or administered law library
119	Produced and/or organized documents
120	Drafted, answered, and assisted with answering an interrogatory
121	Assisted preparation for trial/hearing
122	Researched and/or analyzed public records and hearings

REMINDER: If the sponsor's codes are adopted, attach a copy of the code list and description!

OBJECTIVES
AND GOALS

By contrast, the Weekly Internship Log at Form 3-1 is a weekly recitation both of tasks performed and your own assessment of your strengths and weaknesses. With this design, you will usually see a steady increase in tasks or duties delegated and a corresponding decrease in anxiety. What was once a frightful assignment becomes a routine exercise.

Form 3-1[18]

Intern Name_____Date_____

Weekly Internship Log

Directions: Logs are a reflection of both objectives and task attainment. A successful internship requires a continuous review of the intern's activities. Please note specifically those activities in the following fashion:

Weekly Time Period_____	
Tasks Performed	Strengths and Weaknesses
1.	1.
2.	2.
3.	3.
4.	4.

Weekly Time Period_____	
Tasks Performed	Strengths and Weaknesses
1.	1.
2.	2.
3.	3.
4.	4.

CHAPTER 3

Measuring Specific Paralegal Traits

As an intern you should not only evaluate the global, broad-based internship context but also focus on how you handle individual tasks or functions, problems, and acquired competencies. The types of situations commonly witnessed in the law firm environment, business setting, or in a government agency, should be evaluated from initial performance to finalized accomplishment. Following are some of the skills and functions you will likely master.

Because lawyering, paralegalism, and the justice system exist as a result of disputes, the paralegal needs to have the capacity to live within this conflict and promote resolution rather than contention. Let's say a disgruntled spouse comes into the law firm and says, "That bum husband of mine left me for a 25-year-old flight attendant!"

Problem Resolution

For most interns, a troubled spouse is a disturbing first experience. Obviously, the novice paralegal will be entrapped by all this emotionalism, while the more experienced, seasoned paralegal will temper any judgment about that "bum husband" until all the facts are in. In any event, the paralegal must forge a standard operating procedure that addresses and provides a resolution mechanism. The enormous variations in internship situations may be seen in Figure 3-13.

Figure 3-13

Problem Resolution

An intern has been asked to consider and resolve the following:

Problem: The client wants a preprinted, simple will with fill-in blanks.
Resolution: Give the client a simple will form.

Problem: The client wants a will that will shield a spouse from all tax liability.
Resolution: Assist the attorney in the researching and drafting of a will with multiple trusts or elective share design.

Problem: The client wants all business assets to remain outside of a will, yet still be devised to the remaining spouse.
Resolution: Research turning business assets into a foreign corporation that is exempt from U.S. probate laws.

Problem: The client is gay and wants all Social Security benefits to go to the surviving partner.
Resolution: Advise the client law does not permit this. File an appeal or challenge in federal court.

These examples represent the many avenues for problem resolution and the diversity of problems faced by paralegals. Creativity, adaptability, and tenacity are paralegal traits conducive to problem solving.

OBJECTIVES AND GOALS

Competency Analysis

Another method of measuring one's success at assigned tasks is a step-by-step analysis of the act itself. How does one know when a particular skill or responsibility has been mastered? Each skill, each competency, requires a step-by-step performance analysis.

Stephan Yelon and John Desmedt have created a general step model for use in skill acquisition. See Figure 3-14.

Figure 3-14[19]

Skill Acquisition

Identify the goal.
The paralegal starts with a goal in mind and is alert to certain situational patterns.

Identify and classify the situation by observing the relevant factors.
The paralegal observes the situation and classifies it.

Select the mode.
Based on principles for selecting procedures, the paralegal chooses a procedure likely to achieve the goal.

Adapt or modify the mode.
The paralegal chooses a variant of the procedure based on operating principles.

Perform.
The paralegal acts.

Record efficiency for future use.
The paralegal notes how well the performance succeeded.

Troubleshoot.
When appropriate, the paralegal recognizes an error pattern and considers the likely cause of the problem based on specific operating principles. If there is a problem, the paralegal modifies the goal and/or procedure based on situational and operating principles. The paralegal recognizes the situation that shows completion of the task.

CHAPTER 3

Paralegals can apply these standards easily. Examine the following scenario:

Problem:
>You are requested to come to the office of your supervising attorney, who hands you litigation papers and says, "Serve them."

Resolution:
>Consider the type of service necessary: sheriff, private process service, or mail option. Review the rules of service.
>
>Because it is a federal case with an out-of-state defendant, you look at Federal Rules of Civil Procedure, Rules 4 through 6.
>
>You decide to send them by certified mail.
>
>You await receipt of certified delivery, note time of service, and advise your supervisor.
>
>If the last address is inaccurate or defendant refuses to sign, consider service by publication or hiring a tracing and skip service.

This step-by-step analytical method can be utilized in any job skill analysis, whether it is service of legal documents or preparation of legal pleadings.

Client Counseling

Paralegals earn their stripes on many fronts. They are increasingly asked to conduct interviews, collect data, and serve as a daily liaison with their supervising attorney. By their nature, paralegals free up overwhelmed lawyers. Hence, the capacity to interview and conduct initial client consultation is a crucial competency for any paralegal. Client counseling is a skill learned over time. Entry-level paralegals experience predictable anxiety, while more mature professionals interview with a relaxed demeanor. Employ the Client Counseling Checklist in Form 3-2 to assess your level of comfort during all stages of the internship.

For more information on client interviewing, read Michael Pener's *DISCOVERY: Interviewing and Investigation*, 2d ed. (1995) published by Pearson Publications Co.

76

**OBJECTIVES
AND GOALS**

Form 3-2 [20]

Intern Name_____Date_____

Self-Assessment of Client Counseling Skills

For each of the following skills, please mark the appropriate column that best describes your present degree of comfort.

Skill	Degree of Comfort				
	Highly Uncomfortable	Most Uncomfortable	Uncomfortable	Somewhat Uncomfortable	Comfortable
Paralegal's role as Interviewer					
Paralegal's status/ occupation when compared to a client					
Ability to deal with this type of conflict					
Ability to help others solve problems					

(continued)

CHAPTER 3

Form 3-2 (continued)

Counseling Checklist		
Overall Assessment	**Yes**	**No**
Was my client able to identify the problem?		
Was my client able to identify the direction he/she wanted to go?		
Did I listen?		
Did I look my client in the eye during the discussion?		
Did I try to help my client become more responsible for his/her behavior?		
Did the client choose a problem-solving strategy?		
Could the client identify the resolution?		
Did the interview produce a positive climate?		

Conclusion

The stage is set and ready for your internship to commence. By now, you have formulated a set of goals and objectives, such as a compensated or uncompensated position in a law firm or corporation, post-placement, etc.

You have been fully apprised of the procedural obligations that will arise in the academic environment, from evaluation documents to grading policy, from attendance to report preparation. These goals and objectives are critical components of any successful internship experience.

You have become comfortable with the job description, as well as the many tasks, duties, and obligations seen in the world of paralegalism.

Finally, you have surveyed your level of expectations, from the job to the tasks assigned, weighing their realism or lack thereof, and attempting to keep perspective.

Now let's turn our attention to the ethical considerations that will arise during your internship.

OBJECTIVES AND GOALS

Endnotes

1. San Francisco State University, Paralegal Studies Certificate Program.
2. Mount Vernon Nazarene College, Mount Vernon, OH, Internship Policies and Procedures (1992-93).
3. American Institute for Paralegal Studies, Inc., Southfield, MI 48075.
4. American Institute for Paralegal Studies, Inc., Southfield, MI 48075.
5. American Institute for Paralegal Studies, Inc., Southfield, MI 48075.
6. The Findings of the Competency Committee Relating To: The Quality of Paralegal Services. Copyright 1989. Illinois Paralegal Association, P. O. Box 8089 Bartlett, IL 60103.
7. The Findings of the Competency Committee Relating To: The Quality of Paralegal Services. Copyright 1989. Illinois Paralegal Association, P. O. Box 8089 Bartlett, IL 60103.
8. The Findings of the Competency Committee Relating To: The Quality of Paralegal Services. Copyright 1989. Illinois Paralegal Association, P. O. Box 8089 Bartlett, IL 60103.
9. The Findings of the Competency Committee Relating To: The Quality of Paralegal Services. Copyright 1989. Illinois Paralegal Association, P. O. Box 8089 Bartlett, IL 60103.
10. American Institute for Paralegal Studies, Inc., Southfield, MI 48075.
11. American Institute for Paralegal Studies, Inc., Southfield, MI 48075.
12. American Institute for Paralegal Studies, Inc., Southfield, MI 48075.
13. Michael Milstein, et al. *Internship Programs in Educational Administration: A Guide to Preparing Educational Leaders*, 103 (1991), Teachers College Press, Columbia Univ.
14. Gary R. Gordon and R. Bruce McBride, *Criminal Justice Internships* 26, 2d ed., (1990), Anderson Pub. Co.
15. American Institute for Paralegal Studies, Inc., Southfield, MI 48075.
16. American Institute for Paralegal Studies, Inc., Southfield, MI 48075.
17. American Institute for Paralegal Studies, Inc., Southfield, MI 48075.
18. Waynesburg College, Waynesburg, PA 15370, Internship Program.
19. Stephen Yelon and John Desmedt, Improving Professional Judgment and Performance Training for Open Job Skills, 27 *Performance and Instruction* 34,36 (1988).
20. Michael Milstein, et al. *Internship Programs in Educational Administration: A Guide to Preparing Educational Leaders*, 120 (1991), Teachers College Press, Columbia Univ.

CHAPTER 3

CHAPTER 4

ETHICAL CONSIDERATIONS

The Ethical Framework

The level of ethical rigor applied to those in the legal profession is quite high. Like lawyers, paralegals find a series of professional demands imposed upon them by the nature of the profession, as well as ethical and legal guidelines promulgated by regulatory authorities, bar associations and professional organizations.

Ethical standards are essential to the profession's development and integrity. Deborah Orlik's book, *Ethics for the Legal Assistant*, emphasizes the connection between ethics and professionalism:

> Ethics is a subject which is on everyone's mind today. There are committees to investigate ethics in the judiciary, in law enforcement agencies, in government, in almost every conceivable place. There are research groups across the country dedicated to the study of ethics. Even in light of what we see on the news and read in the newspapers, which may lead us to believe that the world as a whole is "unethical," it is possible to find a predominance of ethical action within the area of legal representation. Not only is it possible to find it, but it is imperative for legal assistants to have it if their profession is to succeed.[1]

Among attorneys, the American Bar Association is the primary player in ethical regulation through its *Model Rules of Professional Conduct*. Paralegal activity is explicitly and vicariously affected by these documents. Take as an illustration Model Rule 5.3, Responsibilities Regarding Nonlawyer Assistants:

> With respect to a nonlawyer employed or retained by or associated with a lawyer:
>
> (a) a partner in a law firm shall make reasonable efforts to ensure that the firm has in effect measures giving reasonable assurance that the person's conduct is compatible with the professional obligations of the lawyer;
>
> (b) a lawyer having direct supervisory authority over the nonlawyer shall make reasonable efforts to ensure that the person's conduct is compatible with the professional obligations of the lawyer; and
>
> (c) a lawyer shall be responsible for conduct of such a person that would be in violation of the rules of professional conduct if engaged in by a lawyer if:

CHAPTER 4

(1) the lawyer orders or, with the knowledge of the specific conduct, ratifies the conduct involved; or

(2) the lawyer is a partner in the law firm in which the person is employed, or has direct supervisory authority over the person, and knows of the conduct at a time when its consequences can be avoided or mitigated but fails to take reasonable remedial action.[2]

The hallmark of Rule 5.3 is its affirmation that final responsibility for any case, and its many related functions, lies with the supervising attorney. Lawyers who delegate, without assumption of the ultimate responsibility, act without an ethical compass.

Model Rule 1.7 on Conflict of Interest: General Rule, gives inferential guidance on how paralegals might trigger a conflict during lawyer/client engagement:

(a) A lawyer shall not represent a client if the representation of that client will be directly adverse to another client, unless:

(1) the lawyer reasonably believes the representation will not adversely affect the relationship with the other client; and

(2) each client consents after consultation.

(b) A lawyer shall not represent a client if the representation of that client may be materially limited by the lawyer's responsibilities to another client or to a third person, or by the lawyer's own interests, unless:

(1) the lawyer reasonably believes the representation will not be adversely affected; and

(2) the client consents after consultation. When representation of multiple clients in a single matter is undertaken, the consultation shall include explanation of the implications of the common representation and the advantages and risks involved.[3]

By their previous associations, the employees of lawyers can instigate various conflicts of interest. Despite diligent efforts to control the conduct of paralegals by controlling lawyers' actions, more direct supervision has long been called for. Even the ABA recognizes the inadequacy of traditional lawyer discipline. Hence, in 1991, at its annual convention, a series of "recommendations submitted to the delegates at the ABA annual meeting in August were the final revision of draft

ETHICAL CONSIDERATIONS

guidelines circulated to more than 80 ABA committees, including the Standing Committees on Ethics and Professional Responsibility, Professional Discipline, and Lawyers Responsibility for Client Protection."[4]

The internship setting will surely prompt an internal review of these and other guidelines. Sometimes unethical employment results from inadvertence or ignorance. The Association of Trial Lawyers of America (ATLA) appreciates the new ethical frontier involving paralegals. A recent article states the following:

> The private practice of law in America is undergoing extraordinary changes that will have a lasting impact on the way lawyers work. Attorneys are now facing the reality that the law is a business as well as a profession. Increased use of paralegals and legal assistants, for example, is carrying law firms in uncharted directions.[5]

As you begin your career as a paralegal, you will want to become thoroughly familiar with all the guidelines for professional behavior set out by the following three organizations: National Association of Legal Assistants (NALA), National Federation of Paralegal Associations (NFPA), and the American Bar Association (ABA). We'll begin with NALA.

National Association Of Legal Assistants

The National Association of Legal Assistants (NALA) has published *Model Standards and Guidelines for Utilization of Legal Assistants.* Review its provisions in Figure 4-1.

Figure 4-1[6]

Model Standards and Guidelines for Utilization of Legal Assistants

Standards and Guidelines for Utilization of Legal Assistants as proposed by the National Association of Legal Assistants 1516 S. Boston, Suite 200, Tulsa, OK 74119. Copyright 1984, revised 1991. Reprinted with permission.

PREAMBLE
Proper utilization of the services of legal assistants affects the efficient delivery of legal services. Legal assistants and the legal profession should be assured that some measures exist for identifying legal assistants and their role in assisting attorneys in the delivery of legal services. Therefore, the National Association of Legal Assistants, Inc., hereby adopts these Model Standards and Guidelines as an educational document for the benefit of legal assistants and the legal profession.

DEFINITION
Legal assistants are a distinguishable group of persons who assist attorneys in the delivery of legal services. Through formal education, training, and experience, legal assistants have knowledge and

(continued)

CHAPTER 4

Figure 4-1 (continued)

expertise regarding the legal system and substantive and procedural law which qualify them to do work of a legal nature under the supervision of an attorney.

STANDARDS

A legal assistant should meet certain minimum qualifications. The following standards may be used to determine an individual's qualifications as a legal assistant:

1. Successful completion of the Certified Legal Assistant (CLA) examination of the National Association of Legal Assistants, Inc.;
2. Graduation from an ABA approved program of study for legal assistants;
3. Graduation from a course of study for legal assistants which is institutionally accredited but not ABA approved, and which requires not less than the equivalent of 60 semester hours of classroom study;
4. Graduation from a course of study for legal assistants, other than those set forth in (2) and (3) above, plus not less than six months of in-house training as a legal assistant;
5. A baccalaureate degree in any field, plus not less than six months in-house training as a legal assistant;
6. A minimum of three years of law-related experience under the supervision of an attorney, including at least six months of in-house training as a legal assistant; or
7. Two years of in-house training as a legal assistant.

For purposes of these standards, "in-house training as a legal assistant" means attorney education of the employee concerning legal assistant duties and these guidelines. In addition to review and analysis of assignments, the legal assistant should receive a reasonable amount of instruction directly related to the duties and obligations of the legal assistant.

GUIDELINES

These guidelines relating to standards of performance and professional responsibility are intended to aid legal assistants and attorneys. The responsibility rests with an attorney who employs legal assistants to educate them with respect to the duties they are assigned and to supervise the manner in which such duties are accomplished.

Legal assistants should:

1. Disclose their status as legal assistants at the beginning of any professional relationship with a client, other attorneys, a court or administrative agency or personnel thereof, or members of the general public;
2. Preserve the confidences and secrets of all clients; and
3. Understand the attorney's Code of Professional Responsibility and these guidelines to avoid any action which would involve the attorney in a violation of that Code, or give the appearance of professional impropriety.

ETHICAL CONSIDERATIONS

Figure 4-1 (continued)

Legal assistants should not:

1. Establish attorney-client relationships; set legal fees; give legal opinions or advice; or represent a client before a court; nor
2. Engage in, encourage, or contribute to any act which could constitute the unauthorized practice of law.

Legal assistants may perform services for an attorney in the representation of a client, provided:

1. The services performed by the legal assistant do not require the exercise of independent professional legal judgment;
2. The attorney maintains a direct relationship with the client and maintains control of all client matters;
3. The attorney supervises the legal assistant;
4. The attorney remains professionally responsible for all work on behalf of the client, including any actions taken or not taken by the legal assistant in connection therewith; and
5. The services performed supplement, merge with, and become the attorney's work product.

In the supervision of a legal assistant, consideration should be given to:

1. Designating work assignments that correspond to the legal assistant's abilities, knowledge, training, and experience;
2. Educating and training the legal assistant with respect to professional responsibility, local rules and practices, and firm policies;
3. Monitoring the work and professional conduct of the legal assistant to ensure that the work is substantively correct and timely performed;
4. Providing continuing education for the legal assistant in substantive matters through courses, institutes, workshops, seminars, and in-house training; and
5. Encouraging and supporting membership and active participation in professional organizations.

Except as otherwise provided by statute, court rule or decision, administrative rule or regulation, or the attorney's Code of Professional Responsibility, and within the preceding parameters and proscriptions, a legal assistant may perform any function delegated by an attorney, including, but not limited to the following:

1. Conduct client interviews and maintain general contact with the client after the establishment of the attorney-client relationship, so long as the client is aware of the status and function of the legal assistant, and the client contact is under the supervision of the attorney;
2. Locate and interview witnesses, so long as the witnesses are aware of the status and function of the legal assistant.
3. Conduct investigations and statistical and documentary research for review by the attorney.
4. Conduct legal research for review by the attorney.
5. Draft legal documents for review by the attorney.

(continued)

CHAPTER 4

Figure 4-1 (continued)

6. Draft correspondence and pleadings for review by and signature of the attorney.
7. Summarize depositions, interrogatories, and testimony for review by the attorney.
8. Attend executions of wills, real estate closings, depositions, court or administrative hearings and trials with the attorney.
9. Author and sign letters provided the legal assistant's status is clearly indicated and the correspondence does not contain independent legal opinions or legal advice.

The *Paralegal Resource Manual* states that "NALA's professional influence is a bold step in outlining minimum requirements of ... experiential, intellectual, and occupational qualification. The summary of tasks and duties that can be performed under the supervision of an attorney are equally important. These guidelines promote acceptable parameters of ethical conduct."[7]

NALA emulates the lawyer's system of canons in its *Code of Ethics and Professional Responsibility*. See the provisions below, which outline similar canons for legal assistants:

> **Canon 1.** A legal assistant shall not perform any of the duties that lawyers only may perform nor do things that lawyers themselves may not do.
>
> **Canon 2.** A legal assistant may perform any task delegated and supervised by a lawyer so long as the lawyer is responsible to the client, maintains a direct relationship with the client, and assumes full professional responsibility for the work product.
>
> **Canon 3.** A legal assistant shall not engage in the practice of law by accepting cases, setting fees, giving legal advice, or appearing in court (unless otherwise authorized by court or agency rules).
>
> **Canon 4.** A legal assistant shall not act in matters involving professional legal judgment as the services of a lawyer are essential in the public interest whenever the exercise of such judgment is required.
>
> **Canon 5.** A legal assistant must act prudently in determining the extent to which a client may be assisted without the presence of a lawyer.

ETHICAL CONSIDERATIONS

Canon 6. A legal assistant shall not engage in the unauthorized practice of law and shall assist in preventing the unauthorized practice of law.

Canon 7. A legal assistant must protect the confidences of a client, and it shall be unethical for a legal assistant to violate any statute now in effect or hereafter to be enacted controlling privileged communications.

Canon 8. It is the obligation of the legal assistant to avoid conduct which would cause the lawyer to be unethical or even appear to be unethical, and loyalty to the employer is incumbent upon the legal assistant.

Canon 9. A legal assistant shall work continually to maintain integrity and a high degree of competency throughout the legal profession.

Canon 10. A legal assistant shall strive for perfection through education in order to better assist the legal profession in fulfilling its duty of making legal services available to clients and the public.

Canon 11. A legal assistant shall do all other things incidental, necessary, or expedient for the attainment of the ethics and responsibilities imposed by statute or rule of court.

Canon 12. A legal assistant is governed by the American Bar Association Model Rules of Professional Conduct.[8]

National Federation of Paralegal Associations

Another influential professional authority that outlines ethical parameters for paralegal conduct is the National Federation of Paralegal Associations (NFPA). Its *Model Code of Ethics and Professional Responsibility* portrays ethical competence as crucial to paralegal performance. See Figure 4-2.

Figure 4-2[9]

Model Code
of Ethics and Professional Responsibility

NFPA recognizes that the creation of guidelines and standards for professional conduct are important for the development and expansion of the paralegal profession. In May 1993, NFPA adopted this Model Code of Ethics and Professional Responsibility ("Model Code") to delineate the principles for ethics and conduct to which every paralegal should aspire. The Model Code expresses NFPA's commitment to increasing the quality and efficiency of legal services and recognizes the profession's responsibilities to the public, the legal community and colleagues.

(continued)

CHAPTER 4

Figure 4-2 (continued)

CANON 1.

A paralegal shall achieve and maintain a high level of competence.

EC-1.1 A paralegal shall achieve competency through education, training, and work experience.

EC-1.2 A paralegal shall participate in continuing education to keep informed of current legal, technical, and general developments.

EC-1.3 A paralegal shall perform all assignments promptly and efficiently.

CANON 2.

A paralegal shall maintain a high level of personal and professional integrity.

EC-2.1 A paralegal shall not engage in any *ex parte* communications involving the courts or any other adjudicatory body in an attempt to exert undue influence or to obtain advantage for the benefit of only one party.

EC-2.2 A paralegal shall not communicate, or cause another to communicate, with a party the paralegal knows to be represented by a lawyer in a pending matter without prior consent of the lawyer representing such other party.

EC-2.3 A paralegal shall ensure that all timekeeping and billing records prepared by the paralegal are thorough, accurate, and honest.

EC-2.4 A paralegal shall be scrupulous, thorough, and honest in the identification and maintenance of all funds, securities, and other assets of a client and shall provide accurate accounting as appropriate.

EC-2.5 A paralegal shall advise the appropriate authority of any dishonest or fraudulent acts by any person pertaining to the handling of funds, securities, or other assets of a client.

CANON 3.

A paralegal shall maintain a high standard of professional conduct.

EC-3.1 A paralegal shall refrain from engaging in any conduct that offends the dignity and decorum of proceedings before a court or other adjudicatory body and shall be respectful of all rules and procedures.

EC-3.2 A paralegal shall advise the proper authority of any action of another legal professional which clearly demonstrates fraud, deceit, dishonesty, or misrepresentation.

EC-3.3 A paralegal shall avoid impropriety and the appearance of impropriety.

CANON 4.

A paralegal shall serve the public interest by contributing to the delivery of quality legal services and the improvement of the legal system.

ETHICAL CONSIDERATIONS

Figure 4-2 (continued)

EC-4.1 A paralegal shall be sensitive to the needs of the public and shall promote the development and implementation of programs that address those needs.

EC-4.2 A paralegal shall support *bona fide* efforts to meet the need for legal services by those unable to pay reasonable and customary fee; for example, participation in *pro bono* projects and volunteer work.

EC-4.3 A paralegal shall support efforts to improve the system and shall assist in making changes.

CANON 5.

A paralegal shall preserve all confidential information provided by the client or acquired from other sources before, during, or after the course of the professional relationship.

EC-5.1 A paralegal shall be aware of and abide by all legal authority governing confidential information.

EC-5.2 A paralegal shall not use confidential information to the disadvantage of the client

EC-5.3 A paralegal shall not use confidential information to the advantage of the paralegal or of a third person.

EC-5.4 A paralegal may reveal confidential information only after full disclosure and with the client's written consent; or when necessary to prevent the client from committing an act which could result in death or serious bodily harm.

EC-5.5 A paralegal shall keep those individuals responsible for the legal representation of a client fully informed of any confidential information the paralegal may have pertaining to the client.

EC-5.6 A paralegal shall not engage in any indiscreet communication concerning clients.

CANON 6.

A paralegal's title shall be filly disclosed.

EC-6.1 A paralegal's title shall clearly indicate the individual's status and shall be disclosed in all business and professional communications to avoid misunderstandings and misconceptions about the paralegal's role and responsibilities.

EC-6.2 A paralegal's title shall be included if the paralegal's name appears on the business cards, letter head, brochures, directories, and advertisements.

CANON 7.

A paralegal shall not engage in the unauthorized practice of law.

EC-7.1 A paralegal shall comply with the applicable legal authority governing the unauthorized practice of law.

CANON 8.

A paralegal shall avoid conflicts of interest and shall disclose any possible conflict to the employer or client, as well as to the prospective employers of clients.

(continued)

CHAPTER 4

Figure 4-2 (continued)

EC-8.1 A paralegal shall act within the bounds of the law, solely for the benefit of the client, and shall be free of compromising influences and loyalties. Neither the paralegal's personal or business interest, nor those of other clients or third persons, should compromise the paralegal's profes sional judgment and loyalty to the client.

EC-8.2 A paralegal shall avoid conflicts of interest which may arise from previous assignments whether for a present or past employer or client.

EC-8.3 A paralegal shall avoid conflicts of interests which may arise from family relationships and from personal and business relationships.

EC-8.4 A paralegal shall create and maintain an effective record-keeping system that identifies clients, matters, and parties with which the paralegal has worked, to be able to determine whether an actual or potential conflict exists.

EC-8.5 A paralegal shall reveal sufficient non-confidential information about a client or former client to reasonably ascertain if an actual or potential conflict of interest exists.

EC-8.6 A paralegal shall not participate in or conduct work on any matter where a conflict of interest has been identified.

EC-8.7 In matters where a conflict of interest has been identified and the client consents to continue representation, a paralegal should comply fully with the implementation and maintenance of an Ethical Wall.

American Bar Association

The American Bar Association, fully recognizing the staggering growth of paralegals, both in number and occupational responsibilities, has promulgated *ABA Guidelines for the Use of Legal Assistants*. The guidelines state in part the following:

> 1. A lawyer is responsible for all of the professional actions of a legal assistant performing legal assistant services at the lawyer's direction and should take reasonable measures to ensure that the legal assistant's conduct is consistent with the lawyer's obligations under the *ABA Model Rules of Professional Conduct*.

> 2. Provided the lawyer maintains responsibility for the work product, a lawyer may delegate to a legal assistant any task normally performed by the lawyer except those tasks proscribed to one not licensed as a lawyer by statute, court rule, administrative rule or regulation, controlling authority, the *ABA Model Rules of Professional Conduct*, or these Guidelines.

ETHICAL
CONSIDERATIONS

3. A lawyer may not delegate to a legal assistant:
   a) Responsibility for establishing an attorney-client relationship.
   b) Responsibility for establishing the amount of a fee to be charged for a legal service.
   c) Responsibility for a legal opinion rendered to a client.

4. It is the lawyer's responsibility to take reasonable measures to ensure that clients, courts, and other lawyers are aware that a legal assistant, whose services are utilized by the lawyer in performing legal services, is not licensed to practice law.

5. A lawyer may identify legal assistants by name and title on the lawyer's letterhead and on business cards identifying the lawyer's firm.

6. It is the responsibility of a lawyer to take reasonable measures to ensure that all client confidences are preserved by a legal assistant.

7. A lawyer should take reasonable measures to prevent conflicts of interest resulting from a legal assistant's other employment or interests insofar as such other employment or interest would present a conflict of interest if it were that of the lawyer.

8. A lawyer may include a charge for the work performed by a legal assistant in setting a charge for legal services.

9. A lawyer may not split legal fees with a legal assistant nor pay a legal assistant for the referral of legal business. A lawyer may compensate a legal assistant based on the quantity of the legal assistant's work and the value of that work to a law practice, but the legal assistant's compensation may not be contingent, by advance agreement, upon the profitability of the lawyer's practice.

10. A lawyer who employs a legal assistant should facilitate the legal assistant's participation in appropriate continuing education and in pro bono publico activities.[10]

Now that an ethical foundation has been established, our attention turns to particular applications.

CHAPTER 4

Exercises for the Paralegal Intern

As an intern, your ethical conscience may be tested. If you keep in mind the ethical guidelines proposed above, there is usually an answer. Following are a series of exercises on ethics with a cited authority to employ in each case.

EXERCISE #1: THE PARALEGAL FEE

Reference: *ABA Model Guidelines for the Use of Legal Asssistants.*

Situation: The attorney is wrapping up a case and needs to prepare a bill. The attorney says to a paralegal, "Calculate your time separately from mine at a rate of $45.00 per hour." The client receives the law firm's bill and refuses to pay the paralegal's fee, saying "That's included in the legal bill!"

Ethical Query: Can separate charges be made for paralegals?

Conclusion:_____

EXERCISE #2: CONFIDENTIALITY

Reference: *NFPA Model Code of Ethics and Professional Responsibility.*

Situation: A supervising attorney and a paralegal are jointly conducting a client interview. The client asks the attorney to keep all the discussions confidential. The client says, "As my attorney, you must keep this quiet." The paralegal decides to tell a friend the entire story.

Ethical Query: Is paralegal bound to the same confidence as the attorney?

Conclusion:_____

EXERCISE #3: UNAUTHORIZED PRACTICE OF LAW

Reference: *NFPA Model Code of Ethics and Professional Responsibility.*

Situation: A supervising attorney has a Social Security disability client in the office. The attorney has a conflict of scheduling regarding the hearing date. The attorney says to a paralegal, "Will you handle that hearing for me?"

ETHICAL CONSIDERATIONS

Ethical Query: Would paralegal advocacy before the Social Security Administration be unauthorized practice of law?

Conclusion:_____

EXERCISE #4: FEE AGREEMENTS

Reference: *NALA Model Standards and Guidelines for Utilization of Legal Assistants.*

Situation: An extremely busy attorney tells a paralegal intern, "I don't have the time to talk to a new client. Negotiate the representation agreement and fee for me."

Ethical Query: Can paralegals negotiate representation and fee agreements?

Conclusion:_____

EXERCISE #5: COMPETENCY

Reference: *NALA Code of Ethics and Responsibility.*

Situation: A paralegal is asked to prepare an antitrust brief. The paralegal proclaims, "What's antitrust? I know nothing about it!" The lawyer replies, "So what! Do the best you can."

Ethical Query: If a lawyer relies on the subsequent research offered by a paralegal, is there a possible ethical violation?

Conclusion:_____

EXERCISE #6: DISCLOSURE OF PARALEGAL STATUS

Reference: *NALA Code of Ethics and Responsibility.*
Situation: A paralegal interviews a client at the office of the supervising attorney. The paralegal collects all the information and never divulges to client that he or she is a paralegal rather than a lawyer.

Ethical Query: Is there any violation for failure to disclose?

Conclusion:_____

93

CHAPTER 4

EXERCISE #7: LAWYER AND PARALEGAL LIABILITY

Reference: *NALA Code of Ethics and Professional Responsibility.*

Situation: An attorney knows that certain evidence in his or her possession should be handed over to a criminal defendant. The attorney gives the evidence to a paralegal and says, "I have to give it to the defense team, but you don't. Act like you never saw it!"

Ethical Query: Can the paralegal not disclose or send over favorable evidence to a criminal defendant?

Conclusion:_____

EXERCISE #8: ADVERTISING

Reference: *ABA Guidelines for the Use of Legal Assistants.*

Situation: An attorney's new stationery design has at the upper right corner: *Paul Jones, Paralegal.*

Ethical Query: Can letterhead or business cards include paralegal designations?

Conclusion:_____

EXERCISE #9: CONFLICTS OF INTEREST

Reference: *ABA Guidelines for the Use of Legal Assistants.*

Situation: John Palumbo, an experienced, seasoned paralegal, once worked for the firm of Dunno and Dunno. A client, one Ronnie Kicko, was once represented by that firm for drug dealing and forgery. John has since taken a new position at the prosecutor's office. Kicko is charged with similar offenses, and John has been assigned to work on the case by the chief prosecutor.

Ethical Query: Does the assignment pose a conflict of interest?

Conclusion:_____

ETHICAL
CONSIDERATIONS

EXERCISE #10: LAWYER SUPERVISION

Reference: *ABA Guidelines for the Use of Legal Assistants.*

Situation: A lawyer tells the new intern, "See this case? It's your problem; I don't want to hear about it. You take care of it!"

Ethical Query: Is this an ethical delegation?

Conclusion:_____

Conclusion: Finding Your Way Through the Ethical Jungle

The preceding exercises should help you evaluate the ethical climate at your sponsoring organization. If you are beginning your internship with the hope that it might lead to permanent employment, these ethical dilemmas and your resolution of them will sharpen your ability to choose a work environment that suits your own sensibilities and does not compromise the standards of legal professionals.

The appendix that follows Chapter 7 contains the answers to the ethical queries.

Endnotes

1. Deborah K. Orlik, *Ethics for the Legal Assistant*, 3rd ed., Marlen Hill Publishing: Encino, CA.
2. *ABA Model Rules of Professional Conduct*, Rule 5.3 (1994).
3. *ABA Model Rules of Professional Conduct*, Rule 1.7 (1994).
4. Note, "ABA Adopts Model Guidelines for Use of Legal Assistants," *Legal Assistant Today* (Nov./Dec. 1991).
5. Association of Trial Lawyers of America, ATLA's Paralegal Affiliates Grow in Numbers, 19 *Advocacy* 15 (March 1993).
6. *NALA Model Standards and Guidelines for Utilization of Legal Assistants* (1991).
7. Charles P. Nemeth, *Paralegal Resource Manual*, Vol. II, 44, 2d ed. (1994), Anderson Pub. Co.
8. *Code of Ethics and Professional Responsibility of National Association of Legal Assistants*, 1516 S. Boston, Suite 200, Tulsa, OK 74119. Copyright 1975, revised 1979, 1988. Reprinted with permission.
9. *NFPA Model Code of Ethics and Professional Responsibility* (1993).
10. "ABA Adopts Model Guidelines for Use of Legal Assistants," *Legal Assistant Today* 12, 13-16 (Nov./Dec. 1991).

CHAPTER 4

CHAPTER 5

ROLE, TASKS, AND OBLIGATIONS

Defining your role as an intern directly correlates to your performance in that role. If interns were mere observers, passively absorbing what others do, there would be little to say. Instead interns are active participants who take on set responsibilities and tasks. It is by doing that paralegals earn their stripes, and their participation is what makes them a priceless part of the legal system. This chapter's approach centers on how your internship experience will unfold, from general guidelines to specific exercises.

Stage I: Listen and Observe

Your introduction to the internship location should be gradual. You are entering the internship phase not because of your expertise, but because of your eagerness, yearning for knowledge, and need for skill enhancement.

You should be extremely observant. Much of what is done in the legal system can be learned through observation alone. Consider these activities:

> how paralegals respond to correspondence
> how discovery, depositions, and interrogatories are done
> how legal research is conducted
> how legal software functions
> how legal papers are served
> how litigation takes place
> how lawyers, judges, and other court personnel conduct
>   themselves
> how pleadings are prepared
> how a law office is administered
> how legal files are maintained
> how legal decisions are appealed.

Don't rush learning by demanding immediate assignments. In the first phase of the internship, you should observe and absorb the activities you will soon be engaged in.

Watching must be coupled with listening. To listen is to learn, so let's illustrate the listening function.

First, ask your supervisor for an explicit job description and listen carefully. If you understand your function precisely, neither you nor your supervisor will have unrealistic expectations.

As your supervisor explains, in exact terms, what your functions will be, listen closely and abide by the parameters set out. Listen to the rules of conduct promul-

97

CHAPTER 5

gated by your sponsor. Every work site has both formal and informal rules of operation and conduct. Listen intently when the supervisor categorizes acceptable and unacceptable behavior.

Listen attentively to policies, standards, and operating procedures, involving everything from copy machines to sexual harassment complaints. The workplace environment the intern enters is markedly different from the academic world. Learn to live within its confines, because you are still only a guest. Pay attention to your supervisor's suggestions and comments in these areas:

> job responsibilities
> chain of command
> office policies
> schedule times
> specific job instructions
> suggestions for correction and improvement
> professional/career advice
> rules of conduct.

At this preliminary stage, you will begin to adjust to the site you have chosen and the job you are assigned. Now you are ready to combine your observational skills with hands-on experience.

Stage II: Learn by Doing

After a sufficient orientation period, you are ready for delegated tasks. The difficulty of the task depends on various factors, including your skill level, the confidence of your supervisor, and the complexity of the internship entity. What is certain is that all interns eventually reach a stage where tasks are meted out, and they are expected to accomplish certain ends.

Because an intern is uninitiated, it is wise for the sponsor or supervisor to write down the assignment by memo or letter. The format may be similar to that shown in Figure 5-1.

ROLE, TASKS, AND OBLIGATIONS

Figure 5-1

Sample Assignment

MEMO
To: Intern
From: Supervisor
Re: Assignment
Date:

Please research the Pennsylvania Business Corporation Law for information on the following topics:

incorporation
private service companies as registered agents
promoters
organizational meeting
directors
issuance of shares

After reviewing your assignment, you may have questions regarding its execution. Instead of personally confronting the supervisor, draft a memo seeking clarification. Do not embark on the assignment until it is thoroughly understood. For a memo design, see Figure 5-2.

Figure 5-2

Sample Memo Response

MEMO

To: Supervisor
From: Intern
Re: Assignment
Date:

Further clarification is needed to complete the research on the Pennsylvania Business Corporation Law assigned to me. I would like to know what type of corporation you wish researched: stock, non-stock, foreign, etc. Thank you.

Don't be afraid to ask questions. Your intern position is, by its very nature, one of inexperience. You should not feel embarrassed or nervous about asking questions. It is better to err on the side of caution than plunge in unprepared.

CHAPTER 5

When an assignment is completed, submit a Status Report to your supervisor. The Status Report, shown in Form 5-1, states the condition of the exercise, whether completed or not, any problems that may have cropped up during its undertaking, and whether the intern has any final recommendations on the exercise's execution.

Form 5-1

Intern Name_____Date_____

Report on Status of Assignment

Today's Date: _____

Date assigned: _____

Assignment No.: _____

Assignment description: _____

_____

_____

Status: Completed____ In progress____ Delayed____

Problems: _____

_____

_____

Recommendations: _____

_____

_____

Aside from daily logs or diaries, explained fully in Chapter Three, you should catalog all assignments, by their exact nature, on a daily or weekly basis. The format suggested at Form 5-2 lists activities by legal topic.

**ROLE, TASKS,
AND OBLIGATIONS**

Form 5-2

Intern Name_____Date_____

Activities Catalog

Topic	Client Code	Description	Time	Expense

10 - Conference

20 - Telephone Conference

30 - Correspondence Review

40 - Correspondence Preparation

50 - Legal Research

60 - Investigation

70 - Document Review

80 - Document Preparation/Assembly

90 - Office Filing

100 - Observation of Legal Proceeding

CHAPTER 5

Our coverage now turns to specific, well-defined tasks that may be encountered in your internship.

Intern Activities

The diversity of intern experiences reflects the variety of approaches to the practice of law. What follows are representative exercises according to practice areas such as real estate and litigation. Use the activity pages to track the task.

Commercial and Consumer Law

Contract disputes, trouble between merchants, warranty claims, and other consumer remedies are always seen in law firms or select government agencies. "Lemon law" litigation charged against American or foreign auto makers will surely be seen by the paralegal. Perform the tasks listed in Form 5-3 by completing the Lemon Law client questionnaire:

Lemon Law

Form 5-3[1]

Intern Name_____Date_____

Client Information Sheet

1. Plaintiff's Full Name: _____
   Residence Address: _____
   Telephone Number: (Home) _____ (Office) _____
2. Spouse's Full Name:_____
   Residence Address: _____
   Telephone Number: (Home) _____ (Office) _____
3. Manufacturer Full Name: _____
4. Manufacturer Local Zone Office Address: _____
5. Dealer Name: _____
6. Dealer Address: _____
7. Date of Purchase: _____
8. Type of Vehicle: _____
9. Vehicle ID No. : _____
10. Date of Delivery Taken: _____
11. Purchase Price: _____ $_____
12. License, registration, and title fees: _____ $_____
13. Sales taxes: _____ $_____
14. Extended Service Plan? _____
15. Other Point-of-Sale Payments (Specify):
    _____ $_____
    _____ $_____
    _____ $_____

**ROLE, TASKS,
AND OBLIGATIONS**

Form 5-3 (continued)

16. Equipment Added After Delivery:
    (a)_____ $_____
    (b)_____ $_____
    (c)_____ $_____
    (d)_____ $_____
    (e)_____ $_____
    (f)_____ $_____

17. Description of Nonconformity:
    No. 1: _____
    No. 2: _____
    No. 3: _____

18. Number of Repairs/Days Out of Service:
    (a) Number of unsuccessful repair attempts for same defect (provide repair order numbers and date[s]): _____
    _____
    _____

    (b) Number of days out of service (provide RO No. and dates):
    _____
    _____
    _____

19. Dealer Service Employees Involved:
    Name/Title/Statements Made:

    _____
    _____
    _____
    _____

    Name/Title/Statements Made:

    _____

20. Manufacturer Employee Involved:
    Name/Title/Statements Made:

    _____
    _____
    _____
    _____

CHAPTER 5

Form 5-3 (continued)

21. Name of Arbitrator: _____
    Date of Decision: _____
    Copy of Arbitration Decision Received? _____
22. Special Instructions:

_____

_____

_____

_____

_____

Letter of Request   Draft a letter outlining a request for repairs, according to the industry standard,
for Repairs   similar to the one in Figure 5-3.

Figure 5-3

Request for Repairs

_____, 19 _____

_____[name of manufacturer]
_____[address]
_____ lcity, state, zip code]

Dear _____ ,

On_____ , our client, _____ , purchased a _____ ,
Vehicle Identification Number _____ . Starting on _____ our
client unceasingly experienced the following malfunction(s):
[LIST VEHICLE MALFUNCTION(S)]
Considering the age of the car and the accumulated mileage, we have been informed that:
[STATE REASON FOR MALFUNCTION(S)]
In accordance with_____ , my client is respectfully requesting repairs,
at your expense, to bring the vehicle up to current industry standards.

Thank you for your immediate attention to this matter.

Sincerely,

Attorney

[Client's Name]

[Client's Signature]

ROLE, TASKS, AND OBLIGATIONS

Domestic Relations

The typical general practice law firm relies heavily on the law of domestic relations. With escalating divorce rates, lawyers are contentious about support and custody issues. Because of the increasing regularity of these types of cases and standardization in forms, most firms have a steady stream of billable hours. Paralegals carry the brunt of administration and data collection.

Client Interview

Conduct a client interview for divorce, employing Form 5-4 below.

Form 5–4[2]

Intern Name_____Date_____

Checklist for Divorce

A. <u>General information</u>
- Client's name, residence address, and telephone number (including maiden and former names if previously married).
- Mailing address of client (may need to suggest opening post office box to preserve confidentiality).
- Business address and telephone number, including FAX number.
- Length of residence in the state.
- Name, residence address, and telephone number of other party.
- Dates and places of birth (each party).
- Status of each party's health (physical and emotional).
- Presence of sexually transmitted diseases.
- Employment history of the parties, including current income and perquisites.
- Date and place of marriage.
- Name of opposing counsel.
- Names of other attorneys with whom our client has consulted.
- Existence of prenuptial or postnuptial agreement.
- Date of separation and which party left the family residence.
- Prior marriages of each party and details of termination.
- Children of prior marriages and custodial arrangements.
- Financial obligations (or rights) from prior marriages.
- Educational backgrounds of each party.
- Contributions of each party as homemaker or to the career enhancement of the other.
- Whether wife is pregnant.
- Counseling and therapy history, if any, and any prior separations or court action.
- Abuse — physical, mental, or drug.
- Any facts warranting injunctive relief.
- Client's objectives (divorce, legal separation, reconciliation) and other party's objectives.
- Behavioral patterns of the parties towards each other.
- Grounds for divorce or other relief.

CHAPTER 5

Form 5-4 (continued)

Children
- Names, dates of birth, and educational status of children.
- Educational plans.
- Physical or emotional problems of children.
- Party with whom children are residing.
- Religious issues.

B. <u>Financial information</u>
- Employment and income history and potential of each party.
- Income of each party from sources other than employment and expectancies.
- Expenses/budget.
- Life insurance of each party (whether term or straight life; what is surrender value, if applicable).
- Each party's assets, including marital, nonmarital, separate, community, and quasicommunity property.
- Pension plans, collectibles, receivables, life insurance cash value, and income tax refund.
- Joint assets of the parties.
- Identification and tracing of nonmarital or separate property of each party.
- Income and other assets of the children, with identities of custodians or trustees.
- Current and potential liabilities of each of the parties, individually and jointly, including tax liabilities, credit cards, etc.
- If either party is self-employed or in business: identity of business or profession, product or service, stock ownership, number and identity of shareholders, partners, directors and/or officers, identity of CPA, and interest of the other party.
- Safe-deposit boxes, location, contents, and party having access.
- Manner of handling family finances.
- Manner in which household and family bills are paid and whether spouse and children receive adequate support.
- Financial records and their location.
- Any threats to transfer or hide assets.

C. <u>Information the client needs to consider</u>
- Dating.
- Signing of anything presented by spouse without consulting the attorney, especially a tax return.
- Assuming all conversations with spouse being taped.
- The right to temporary and injunctive relief.
- The right to a restraining order.
- Experts — types, cost, and who hires.
- Private investigator.
- Reconsidering life insurance benefits and will.
- Court requirements of mediation, seminars, or appointment of guardian *ad litem*.
- Child support and visitation may be modifiable.
- Alimony modifiable unless specified otherwise.
- Equitable division.
- Child support guidelines.
- Changes in assets outside of course of ordinary business affairs.
- No-fault divorce.

Reprinted with permission of Michie Butterworth, © 1991

ROLE, TASKS, AND OBLIGATIONS

File
Papers

To put the guidelines into practice, conduct the following exercise:

Your supervisor has just handed you a Motion to Modify Support, saying, "File it!" Answer these questions:

Place of filing?

Whom filed with?

How many copies?

Other parties getting copy?

Any filing costs?

If so, how much?

Real Estate

Another workhorse area for the law firm is real estate. Whether buying or selling, both sides need legal assistance.

Agreement of Sale

Utilize the checklist in either Form 5-5 or Form 5-6 in a client consultation.

Form 5-5[3]

Intern Name_____ Date_____

Checklist for Agreement of Sale (Buyer's Version)

I. Seller
*   Confirm the seller's name, address, and telephone numbers.
*   Ascertain the legal status of seller(s).
*   If a corporation, ascertain the state of incorporation.
*   If a partnership, is it general or limited and list the names of the individuals.
*   If the sellers are husband and wife, do they both approve of the sale? Was the marriage terminated?
*   If a single person, was he or she married at the time the title was acquired? Was the single person married at any time thereafter the title was acquired?
*   If an executor or administrator, obtain proof of authority to sell.

CHAPTER 5

Form 5-5 (continued)

II. Buyer
- Confirm the buyer(s) name, address, and telephone numbers.
- Ascertain the manner in which buyer(s) will take and hold title:
  - as a partnership in the partnership name
  - as a partnership in the individual names of the partners and their spouses, as joint tenants with rights of survivorship, tenants in common, or otherwise
  - as husband and wife as tenants by the entireties
  - as a single person(s)
- Ascertain the purpose for property purchase:
  - buyer's residence
  - speculation
  - subdivision
  - commercial development
  - other:

III. The Property
- Confirm the location: street, lot number, ward, township, city, county, and state.
- Determine any deed reference or boundaries necessary and describe.
- If a metes and bounds description is available, insert in the agreement of sale.
- If any personal property is to be sold with the land, add an addendum to the agreement, entitle it "Inventory," and list each item.

IV. The Purchase Price and Financing
- Confirm the total purchase price.
- Determine the amount of the downpayment and due date(s).
- Ascertain the manner in which payment of purchase price is to be made at the time of final settlement:
  - assumption of existing mortgage
  - purchase money mortgage
  - cash (no financial arrangements with a lending institution)
- Mortgage contingency clause - If the buyer must obtain a loan commitment for financing the property, indicate the specifics in the mortgage contingency clause.
- Determine who is to retain the downpayment until final closing: the broker, buyer, seller, or attorney.

V. General Considerations
- Confirm the settlement date (on or before).
- Determine from the seller (or the seller's attorney) exactly what personal property owned by the seller is included in the sale, then list each item and the purchase price.
- Determine the amount of insurance the seller is presently carrying on the property and insert it in the agreement of sale.

ROLE, TASKS, AND OBLIGATIONS

Form 5-5 (continued)

- Make sure there is only one remedy in the agreement of sale in case of default by the buyer.
- Obtain a statement as to what use the property is zoned for.
- Confirm that the seller will convey to the buyer a good and marketable title.
- Confirm that there is no pending or threatened condemnation.
- Make sure there are no deed restrictions affecting any portion of the property or any special conditions, exceptions, covenants, or reservations.
- Confirm that the seller has complied with all laws, ordinances, etc., relating to the property.
- Confirm that there is available water, sewer, and electricity for "tap in."
- Confirm that there are no notices of any violation by any governmental unit or agency and that, if there are, the seller will correct said violations at the seller's cost and expense prior to settlement.
- Is there any requisite approval of subdivision planning required? If so, note the dates for the necessary approval.
- Confirm the approval of leases, if any: Are they assignable?
- Confirm the approval or appraisal of the property by the lending institution, F.H.A or V.A.
- Add a termite clause — pro-buyer.
- Confirm that rezoning or issuance of permits is consonant with the use of land.
- Confirm that fuel oil is to be included in the sale and purchase price.
- Is the contract assignable by the buyer(s)?
- Notice provisions — Does the notice have to be received or is mailing adequate?
- Is the successors and assigns clause in the contract?
- If the entire agreement clause is contained, then no parol evidence is allowed.
- Is the severability clause present to prevent failure of entire agreement if one provision is invalid?
- The contract should state that time is of the essence. If silent, performance within a reasonable time will suffice.
- Has the buyer placed any time limit within which the seller must accept the contract?
- Is the signature page acceptable for proper execution?
- Is the agreement of sale dated?
- Were any amendments or modifications to the agreement of sale made? If so, were they made to suffice legally?
- Real estate commissioners — Are the commissions conditioned on the closing of the transaction if not already determined by the listing contract?
- Is the responsible party to the contract listed as the one responsible to pay any real estate commissions?
- Is there representation and warranty by both parties that no other brokers are involved in the transaction?
- Are the breaches of the contract and what constitutes the breaches clearly stated and the remedies to the seller clearly stated?
- Are any surveys to be obtained? If so, by whom? Who is responsible for the costs and expenses of the surveys?
- Is the "not to be recorded clause" in the agreement?
- Special considerations and clauses.

CHAPTER 5

Form 5-6[4]

Intern Name_____Date_____

Checklist for Agreement of Sale (Seller's Version)

I. Seller
*   Confirm the seller's name, address, and telephone numbers.
*   Ascertain the legal status of the seller(s):
    *   If a corporation, ascertain the state of incorporation.
    *   If a partnership holding title in the partnership name, list the partnerships who are authorized to sign a conveyance of the property, i.e., general or limited.
    *   If a partnership holding the title in the individual names of one or more of the partners, list the names of the partners and whether they approve of the sale.
    *   If the sellers are husband and wife, do both approve of the sale?
    *   If the seller is a single person, was the single person married at the time title was acquired or at any time thereafter, and how was the marriage terminated?
    *   If the seller is a surviving joint tenant, how and when was the joint tenancy terminated?
    *   If the seller is an executor or administrator, ascertain the proof of authority to sell.

II. Buyer
*   Confirm the buyer's name, address, and telephone numbers.
*   Confirm the manner in which the buyer(s) will take and hold title:
    *   As a partnership in the partnership name.
    *   As a partnership in the individual names of the partners or the individual names of the partners and their spouses as joint tenants with right of survivorship, tenants in common, or otherwise.
    *   As husband and wife as tenants by the entireties.
    *   As a single person(s).

III. The Property
*   Confirm the location: street, lot number, ward, township, city, county, state.
*   Obtain an inventory or description of any personal property to be sold with the land and attach as an addendum to the agreement of sale.

IV. The Purchase Price and Financing
*   Confirm the total purchase price.
*   Confirm the manner in which the purchase price is to be paid:
    *   The downpayment or other deposit at signing of the agreement of sale and due date.
    *   Assumption of existing mortgage.
    *   Purchase money mortgage.
    *   Cash (no financial arrangements with a lending institution).
    *   Assumption of existing encumbrances on property.
*   Confirm the manner in which payment of the purchase price, if payable in installments, is to be secured.

ROLE, TASKS, AND OBLIGATIONS

Form 5-6 (continued)

V. <u>General Considerations</u>
- Make sure that delivery of vacant property to buyer will be at time of final settlement.
- Obtain approval of the leases, if existing, and assignment of the leases.
- Make sure the buyer obtains a loan or commitment for loans on the property (the mortgage contingency).
- Insert a termite inspection (pro-seller).
- Obtain certification of the zoning classification.
- Confirm the settlement date.
- Confirm the name and location of the broker handling the settlement, if any.
- Make sure the broker's commission is specified.
- Other.

Master Mailing List   Create a master mailing list for the typical real estate transaction using Form 5-7.

Form 5-7

Intern Name_____Date_____

Master Mailing List

	Address	Phone Number
Buyer		
Seller		
Real Estate Agent		
Real Estate Broker		
Pest Inspector		
Surveyor		
Bank or Mortgage Co.		
Title Company		
Attorneys		
Closing Agents		
Paralegals		

CHAPTER 5

Settlement
Sheet

Prepare a preliminary settlement sheet with the following information:

Contract sales price - $260,000.00

Prorata Expenses
City/town taxes - $445.95
County/State taxes - $1,980.90
School tax - $1,639.25

Borrower's Information
Deposit - $5,000.00
Principal amount of new loan - $175,000
Additional funds - $89,000.00
Loan expenses
       document preparation - $100.00
       processing - $250.00
       tax service fee - $90.00
Interest paid in advance to lender - 3/01 to 3/05/94 @ $22.77/day
Settlement fee - $150.00
Title examination - $75.00
Title insurance binder - $25.00
Notary fees - $20.00
Title insurance - $487.50
Charge for endorsements 100 and 300 - $80.00
Overnight delivery charge - $29.00
Recording fees
       deed - $19.50
       mortgage - $23.50
       releases - $31.00
City/county tax/stamps for deed - $2,600.00

Seller's Information
Payoff of first mortgage loan - $66,680.77
Payoff of second mortgage loan - $119,060.70
Commission on contract sales price is 5.28%, divided equally between two brokers
Seller's distribution - $15.00
Overnight delivery - $30.00
State tax/stamps for deed - $2,600.00
Louise Friend is due $2,295.00 from seller
Borough certifications are due in the amount of $40.00
Final water bill - $44.98
Final sewage bill - $93.13

ROLE, TASKS, AND OBLIGATIONS

Use the settlement sheet in Form 5-8.

Form 5-8

Intern Name_____Date_____

Settlement Statement

HUD-1 (03-86) OMB NO. 2502-0265

A.	B. TYPE OF LOAN:
U.S. DEPARTMENT OF HOUSING & URBAN DEVELOPMENT **SETTLEMENT STATEMENT**	1. ☐ FHA 2. ☐ FmHA 3. ☐ CONV. UNINS. 4. ☐ VA 5. ☐ CONV. INS. 6. FILE NUMBER: 7. LOAN NUMBER: 8. MORTGAGE INSURANCE CASE NUMBER:

C. NOTE: *This form is furnished to give you a statement of actual settlement costs. Amounts paid to and by the settlement agent are shown. Items marked "(p.o.c.)" were paid outside the closing; they are shown here for informational purposes and are not included in the totals.*

D. NAME OF BORROWER:	E. NAME OF SELLER:	F. NAME OF LENDER:

G. PROPERTY LOCATION:	H. SETTLEMENT AGENT PLACE OF SETTLEMENT	I. SETTLEMENT DATE:

J. SUMMARY OF BORROWER'S TRANSACTION		K. SUMMARY OF SELLER'S TRANSACTION	
100. GROSS AMOUNT DUE FROM BORROWER:		**400. GROSS AMOUNT DUE TO SELLER:**	
101. Contract sales price		401. Contract sales price	
102. Personal property		402. Personal property	
103. Settlement charges to borrower (line 1400)		403.	
104.		404.	
105.		405.	
Adjustments for items paid by seller in advance		*Adjustments for items paid by seller in advance*	
106. City/town taxes to		406. City/town taxes to	
107. County taxes to		407. County taxes to	
108. Assessments to		408. Assessments to	
109.		409.	
110.		410.	
111.		411.	
112.		412.	
120. GROSS AMOUNT DUE FROM BORROWER		**420. GROSS AMOUNT DUE TO SELLER**	
200. AMOUNTS PAID BY OR IN BEHALF OF BORROWER:		**500. REDUCTIONS IN AMOUNT DUE TO SELLER:**	
201. Deposit or earnest money		501. Excess deposit (see instructions)	
202. Principal amount of new loan(s)		502. Settlement charges to seller (line 1400)	
203. Existing loan(s) taken subject to		503. Existing loan(s) taken subject to	
204.		504. Payoff of first mortgage loan	
205.		505. Payoff of second mortgage loan	
206.		506.	
207.		507.	
208.		508.	
209.		509.	
Adjustments for items unpaid by seller		*Adjustments for items unpaid by seller*	
210. City/town taxes to		510 City/town taxes to	
211. County taxes to		511. County taxes to	
212. Assessments to		512. Assessments to	
213.		513.	
214.		514.	
215.		515.	
216.		516.	
217.		517.	
218.		518.	
219.		519.	
220. TOTAL PAID BY/FOR BORROWER		**520. TOTAL REDUCTION AMOUNT DUE SELLER**	
300. CASH AT SETTLEMENT FROM/TO BORROWER		**600. CASH AT SETTLEMENT TO/FROM SELLER**	
301. Gross amount due from borrower (line 120)		601. Gross amount due to seller (line 420)	
302. Less amounts paid by/for borrower (line 220)		602. Less reductions in amount due seller (line 520)	
303. CASH (☐ FROM) (☐ TO) BORROWER		**603. CASH (☐ TO) (☐ FROM) SELLER**	

The undersigned hereby acknowledge receipt of a completed copy of pages 1 and 2 of this statement and any attachments referred to herein.

Borrower _____   Seller _____

Borrower _____   Seller _____

CHAPTER 5

Form 5-8 (continued)

L. Settlement Charges

	Paid From Borrower's Funds at Settlement	Paid From Seller's Funds at Settlement
700. Total Sales/Broker's Commission Based on Price $ @ % =		
Division of Commission (line 700) As Follows:		
701. $ to		
702. $ to		
703. Commission Paid At Settlement		
704.		
800. Items Payable In Connection With Loan		
801. Loan Origination Fee %		
802. Loan Discount %		
803. Appraisal Fee to		
804. Credit Report to		
805. Lender's Inspection Fee		
806. Mortgage Insurance Application Fee to		
807. Assumption Fee		
808.		
809.		
810.		
811.		
900. Items Required By Lender To Be Paid In Advance		
901. Interest from to @ $ /day		
902. Mortgage Insurance Premium for months to		
903. Hazard Insurance Premium for years to		
904. years to		
905.		
1000. Reserves Deposited With Lender		
1001. Hazard Insurance months @ $ per month		
1002. Mortgage Insurance months @ $ per month		
1003. City Property Taxes months @ $ per month		
1004. County Property Taxes months @ $ per month		
1005. Annual Assessments months @ $ per month		
1006. School Property Taxes months @ $ per month		
1007. months @ $ per month		
1008. months @ $ per month		
1100. Title Charges		
1101. Settlement or Closing Fee to		
1102. Abstract or Title Search to		
1103. Title Examination to		
1104. Title Insurance Binder to		
1105. Document Preparation to		
1106. Notary Fees to		
1107. Attorney's Fees to		
(includes above items numbers:)		
1108. Title Insurance to		
(includes above items numbers:)		
1109. Lender's Coverage $		
1110. Owner's Coverage $		
1111. Endorsements		
1112. Seller's Distribution Fee		
1113.		
1200. Government Recording and Transfer Charges		
1201. Recording Fees: Deed $; Mortgage $; Releases $		
1202. City/County Tax/Stamps: Deed $; Mortgage $		
1203. State Tax/Stamps: Deed $; Mortgage $		
1204.		
1205.		
1300. Additional Settlement Charges		
1301. Survey to		
1302. Pest Inspection to		
1303. Taxes		
1304. Sewer Rent		
1305.		
1400. Total Settlement Charges (enter on lines 103, Section J and 502, Section K)		

To the best of my knowledge, the HUD-1 Settlement Statement which I have prepared is a true and accurate account of the funds which were received and have been or will be disbursed by the undersigned as part of the settlement of this transaction

_____   _____
Settlement Agent   Date

114

**ROLE, TASKS,
AND OBLIGATIONS**

*Criminal
Law*

Interpersonal, evidentiary, and investigative skills are essential for paralegals working with prosecutors, public defenders, and law enforcement personnel.

*Bail
Reduction*

Conduct a bail reduction or elimination interview using Form 5-9 to ascertain the financial status of the defendant.

Form 5-9[5]

Intern Name_____Date_____

Financial Status

1. Marital Status:
    a. Single _____ Married _____ Separated ____ Divorced _____
    b. Dependents: Spouse _____ Children _____ No. of Children _____
       Other Dependents: No. and Relationship _____

2. Residence:
    Address: _____
    Telephone: _____

3. Employment:
    Name of Employer: _____
    Address of Employer: _____
    Telephone No. of Employer: _____
    Period of Employment with Present Employer: _____
    Income: $ _____ per week $_____ month
    Nature of Employment: _____

4. If Married, Spouse's Employment:
    Name of Employer: _____
    Address of Employer: _____
    Telephone No. of Employer: _____
    Income: $ _____ per week $ _____ month
    Nature of Employment: _____

CHAPTER 5

Form 5-9 (continued)

5. Owner of Real Property: Yes _____ No _____
    a. Description: _____
    b. Address: _____
    c. In Whose Name: _____
    d. Estimated Value $ _____
    e. Total Amount Owed $ _____ to _____
    f. Annual Income From Property $ _____

6. Other Property:
    a. Automobile: Make _____ Model _____
       In Whose Name Registered _____
       Present Value of Car $ _____
       Amount Owed $ _____ to _____
    b. Cash on Hand $ _____
       Cash in Banks and Savings and Loan Associations $ _____
       Name and Address of Banks and Associations: _____
       _____
       _____
    c. Other income $ _____

7. Obligations:
    a. Monthly Rental on House or Apartment $ _____
    b. Monthly Mortgage Payments on House $ _____
    c. Other Debts:
       Amount owed $ _____ to _____ Total Monthly Payments on Debts $ _____

Motion for
Continuance

Prepare a motion for continuance based on a lack of legal representation using the pleading format in Figure 5-4.

ROLE, TASKS, AND OBLIGATIONS

Figure 5–4

Motion for Continuance Worksheet

(Title)
Motion for Continuance

Defendant, by his attorney, hereby requests the court that the trial of the above-entitled case, now set for _____ ,19 _____ be continued, by reason: _____
_____

This request is based on the annexed affidavit of _____ ,
all the records and files in this case, and any additional evidence that may be brought forth at the hearing.

Dated _____ , 19 _____ .

(Signature and address)

Robbery or Burglary Location   Prepare a chart or graph that portrays a robbery or burglary location using the template provided on the following page.

CHAPTER 5

Prepare a chart or graph that portrays a robbery or burglary location.

N
W ─── ─── E
S

Key

118

**ROLE, TASKS,
AND OBLIGATIONS**

**Wills,
Trusts,
and Estates**

Paperwork, client counseling, and data collection are all activities of the paralegal working in estates and trusts.

Client Interview

Conduct a client interview dealing with will preparation using Form 5-10.

Form 5-10[6]

Intern Name_____Date_____

Client Interview for Will Preparation

CLIENT INFORMATION PACKAGE

Will Preparation/Estate
    Planning for _____ Date Prepared _____
    File No. _____ Update Due _____

    Home Address _____
    Home Phone _____
    Employer _____
    Business Address _____
    Business Phone _____
    Notes, Comments _____
    _____
    _____

FAMILY INFORMATION

1. Husband:
    a. Full name _____
    b. Date & place of birth/citizenship _____
    c. Social Security Number _____
    d. Prior marriages _____

2. Wife:
    a. Full name _____
    b. Maiden name _____
    c. Date and place of birth/citizenship _____
    d. Social Security Number _____
    e. Prior marriages _____

CHAPTER 5

Form 5-10 (continued)

3. Date and place of marriage:

4. Children: (Indicate if adopted or if from prior marriage.)

	Name & Address	Marital Status	Birthdate/Place
a.			
b.			
c.			
d.			
e.			

5. Grandchildren:

	Names of Grandchildren	Parents' Names	Birthdate
a.			
b.			
c.			
d.			
e.			
f.			
g.			
h.			
i.			

6. Husband's Parents:
   a. Father's Name _____
      Address _____
      Birthdate/Age _____
   b. Mother's Name _____
      Address _____
      Birthdate/Age _____

7. Wife's Parents:
   a. Father's Name _____
      Address _____
      Birthdate/Age _____
   b. Mother's Name _____
      Address _____
      Birthdate/Age _____

8. Do husband and wife contribute to the support of or financially assist any of their parents? _____
   To what extent? _____

**ROLE, TASKS,
AND OBLIGATIONS**

Form 5-10 (continued)

9. Other Dependents:
   Names, addresses, and relationship:
   a. _____
   b. _____
   c. _____
   d. _____

10. Is (was) either spouse a member of the armed services?
    Branch _____
    Serial No. _____
    Current Status _____
    Disability _____

11. Does either spouse belong to any lodge, fraternal organization, etc.?
    Name _____
    Address _____
    Death _____
    Disability or other Benefits _____
    Name _____
    Address _____
    Death _____

CLIENT'S EMPLOYMENT, SOCIAL SECURITY, AND VETERAN'S BENEFITS

1. Employment Benefits:
   a. Pension
      -Company _____
      -Amount Vested, Contributed, Deferred _____
      -Estimated Income or Lump Sum Payment _____
      -Death Benefit _____
   b. Profit Sharing
      -Company _____
      -Amount Vested, Contributed, Deferred _____
      -Estimated Income or Lump Sum Payment _____
      -Death Benefit _____
   c. Thrift Plan, Deferred Compensation
      -Company _____
      -Amount Vested, Contributed, Deferred _____
      -Estimated Income or Lump Sum Payment _____
      -Death Benefit _____

CHAPTER 5

Form 5-10 (continued)

   d. Self-Employment Retirement Plans, IRAs, Keogh Plan
       -Company _____
       -Amount Vested, Contributed, Deferred _____
       -Estimated Income or Lump Sum Payment _____
       -Death Benefit _____
   e. Government Benefits
       -Company _____
       -Amount Vested, Contributed, Deferred _____
       -Estimated Income or Lump Sum Payment _____
       -Death Benefit _____
   f. Other (Specify)
       -Company _____
       -Amount Vested, Contributed, Deferred _____
       -Estimated Income or Lump Sum Payment _____
       -Death Benefit _____

2. Social Security Benefits:
    Description of Benefit _____ Amount Received _____
          a. _____
          b. _____
          c. _____

3. Veteran's Benefits: Account Reg. or Serial Number _____
       a. Pension/Retirement _____
          Amount Received/Anticipated _____
       b. Disability _____
          Amount Received/Anticipated _____
       c. Death _____
          Amount Received/Anticipated _____

4. Other: (Specify) _____

SPOUSE'S EMPLOYMENT, SOCIAL SECURITY, AND VETERAN'S BENEFITS

1. Employment Benefits:
   a. Pension
       -Company _____
       -Amount Vested, Contributed, Deferred _____
       -Estimated Income or Lump Sum Payment _____
       -Death Benefit _____

ROLE, TASKS, AND OBLIGATIONS

Form 5-10 (continued)

    b. Profit Sharing
        -Company _____
        -Amount Vested, Contributed, Deferred _____
        -Estimated Income or Lump Sum Payment _____
        -Death Benefit _____
    c. Thrift Plan, Deferred Compensation
        -Company _____
        -Amount Vested, Contributed, Deferred _____
        -Estimated Income or Lump Sum Payment _____
        -Death Benefit _____
    d. Self-Employment Retirement Plans, IRAs, Keogh Plan
        -Company _____
        -Amount Vested, Contributed, Deferred _____
        -Estimated Income or Lump Sum Payment _____
        -Death Benefit _____
    e. Government Benefits
        -Company _____
        -Amount Vested, Contributed, Deferred _____
        -Estimated Income or Lump Sum Payment _____
        -Death Benefit _____
    f. Other (Specify)
        -Company _____
        -Amount Vested, Contributed, Deferred _____
        -Estimated Income or Lump Sum Payment _____
        -Death Benefit _____

2. Social Security Benefits:

	Description of Benefit	Amount Received
a.	_____	_____
b.	_____	_____
c.	_____	_____

3. Veteran's Benefits: Account Reg. or Serial Number _____
        a. Pension/Retirement _____
           Amount Received/Anticipated _____
        b. Disability _____
           Amount Received/Anticipated _____
        c. Death _____
           Amount Received/Anticipated _____

4. Other: (Specify) _____

CHAPTER 5

Form 5-10 (continued)

FINANCIAL DATA: ASSETS AND LIABILITIES

Cash on Deposit (include Credit Unions):
1. Name(s) of Owners _____
      Type of Account _____
      Account Number _____
      Current Balance _____
      Bank & Address _____
2. Name(s) of Owners _____
      Type of Account _____
      Account Number _____
      Current Balance _____
      Bank & Address _____
3. Name(s) of Owners _____
      Type of Account _____
      Account Number _____
      Current Balance _____
      Bank & Address _____

Certificates of Deposit:

	Face Amount	Rate	Term	Maturity	Date
a.					
b.					
c.					
d.					
e.					

Stocks, Publicly Held:

	Per Share Value	Total	Description	Ownership	No. of Shares	Value
a.						
b.						
c.						
d.						
e.						

ROLE, TASKS, AND OBLIGATIONS

Form 5-10 (continued)

Bonds, Publicly Held:

	Description	Ownership	Face Amt.	Date of Issuance	Maturity Date	Est. Value
a.						
b.						
c.						
d.						

Closely Held Business Interests:
List all stocks and bonds and give all relevant details.
Indicate and describe any buy-sell agreements affecting these interests.

Real Estate:
1. Mailing Address:
    -Legal Description and Mailing Address, include Zip Code _____
    -How Title Held _____
    -Fair Market Value $ _____
    -Date of Maturity _____
    -Mortgaged With (Bank) _____
2. Mailing Address:
    -Legal Description and Mailing Address, include Zip Code _____
    -How Title Held _____
    -Fair Market Value $ _____
    -Date of Maturity _____
    -Mortgaged With (Bank) _____
3. Mailing Address:
    -Legal Description and Mailing Address, include Zip Code _____
    -How Title Held _____
    -Fair Market Value $ _____
    -Date of Maturity _____
    -Mortgaged With (Bank) _____

Automobiles, Recreation Vehicles, Boats:

	Description	Ownership	Fair Market Value	Encumbrance
a.				
b.				
c.				
d.				

Total Value $_____

CHAPTER 5

Form 5-10 (continued)

Household Furnishings:

	Description	Ownership	Fair Market Value
a.			
b.			
c.			
d.			

Total Value $_____

Jewelry:

	Description	Ownership	Fair Market Value
a.			
b.			
c.			
d.			

Total Value $_____

Special Collections (Antiques, Coins, Artwork, etc.):

	Description	Ownership	Fair Market Value
a.			
b.			
c.			
d.			

Total Value $_____

Other Tangible Property:

	Description	Ownership	Fair Market Value
a.			
b.			
c.			
d.			

Total Value $_____

Jointly Held Property Not Otherwise Listed:

	Description	Ownership	Fair Market Value
a.			
b.			
c.			
d.			

Total Value $_____

ROLE, TASKS, AND OBLIGATIONS

Form 5-10 (continued)

Spouse's Assets Not Otherwise Listed:

Description	Ownership	Fair Market Value
a.		
b.		
c.		
d.		

Total Value $_____

Interests in Estates or Trusts:
1. Name _____
   Fiduciary _____
   Interest and Value _____
2. Name _____
   Fiduciary _____
   Interest and Value _____

Other Expectancies:

Description	Fair Market Value
a.	
b.	
c.	
d.	

Gifts:

Have any gifts requiring a Gift Tax Return been made by either spouse? If yes, give dates, amount, and name(s) of donor(s). Attach copies of Gift Tax Returns.

Liabilities (Other than Mortgages):
1. Notes, Loans, and Judgments:

Description	To Whom Paid	Acct. Number	Total Debt
a.			
b.			
c.			
d.			

2. Agreements:

Description	To Whom Paid		Total Debt
a.			
b.			
c.			
d.			

CHAPTER 5

Form 5-10 (continued)

3. Support Orders:

	Description	To Whom Paid	Total Debt
a.			
b.			
c.			
d.			

4. Other Financial Obligations: Provide details

a. _____

b. _____

c. _____

d. _____

ADMINISTRATION AND DISTRIBUTION OBJECTIVES

Questions the client should consider:

1. Whom would you like to serve as Executor or Executrix of your Wills?

   First Choice

   Name _____

   Address _____

   Age _____ Relationship _____

   Second Choice:

   Name _____

   Address _____

   Age _____ Relationship _____

   Is independent administration authorized?

2. In the event that both husband and wife die leaving a child or children under the legal age, whom would you want to serve as guardian?

   First Choice

   Name _____

   Address _____

   Age _____ Relationship _____

   Second Choice:

   Name _____

   Address _____

   Age _____ Relationship _____

ROLE, TASKS, AND OBLIGATIONS

Form 5-10 (continued)

3. If an individual trustee is needed for any reason, whom would you want to serve in that capacity?

   First Choice:
   Name _____
   Address _____
   Age _____ Relationship_____
   Second Choice:
   Name _____
   Address _____
   Age _____ Relationship_____

4. Do you wish to waive the executor's bonding?

5. Upon your death from what source(s) do you want any incurred funeral expenses to be paid?

6. How, and to whom, do you want your primary assets distributed?

7. Will you attach a separate paper listing any valuable or personally significant property and to whom you wish it distributed? (Example: my gold wedding rings to my daughter, Mary Smith.)

8. Do you wish to make any personal cash bequests? State to whom and give details.

9. Do you wish to make bequests to your church or synagogue or to any other charitable organizations? Give details.

10. If you and your spouse die prematurely, should your children receive property at the age of majority or should it be held to a more mature age?

11. Do any of your children or other dependents have special educational, medical, or financial needs?

12. Do you expect that, upon your death, your spouse will be capable of effective financial management?

13. Do you want your spouse to manage your estate from an investment standpoint?

14. To whom would your spouse look for management help?

15. Is avoiding unnecessary estate taxation of any great importance to you?

16. Is minimizing income taxes of great importance to you?

17. Do you contemplate making any substantial gifts in the future? Explain.

CHAPTER 5

Form 5-10 (continued)

18. If none of your children are living at the time of your spouse's death, to whom do you want your estate to go? Your family? Spouse's family? Elsewhere?

19. Does your spouse have employment skills? Do you expect that your survivor will work?

20. Do you expect that your spouse will continue to live in your present home?

ADVISORS' NAMES, ADDRESSES, AND TELEPHONE NUMBERS:

1. Attorney:
2. Accountant:
3. Life Insurance Advisor:
4. Bankers and Trust Officers:
5. Stockbroker:
6. Executor:
7. Trustee:
8. Designated Guardian for Children:
9. Investment Advisor:
10. Physician:
11. Clergyman:

LIFE INSURANCE POLICIES
(Include policies on the life of spouse and children.)

(Proceeds of life insurance policies on a testator pass outside the scope of the will, unless the estate of the testator is the designated beneficiary.)

Provided by Employer: Policy 1   Policy 2   Policy 3
Company _____
Policy _____
Type _____
Insured _____
Owner _____
Beneficiary _____
Contingent Beneficiary _____
Face Value _____
Amount of Loan _____
Employee's Contribution _____

ROLE, TASKS, AND OBLIGATIONS

Form 5-10 (continued)

Other Life Insurance:

Company _____
Policy _____
Type _____
Insured _____
Owner _____
Beneficiary _____
Contingent Beneficiary _____
Face Value _____
Amount of Loan _____
Employee's Contribution _____

MEDICAL AND DISABILITY INSURANCE

Medical:
    Company _____
    Policy or Group Number _____
    Benefits _____
    Beneficiary _____
Surgical:
    Company _____
    Policy or Group Number _____
    Benefits _____
    Beneficiary _____
Hospital:
    Company _____
    Policy or Group Number _____
    Benefits _____
    Beneficiary _____
Disability:
    Company _____
    Policy or Group Number _____
    Benefits _____
    Beneficiary _____
Other:
    Company _____
    Policy or Group Number _____
    Benefits _____
    Beneficiary _____

CHAPTER 5

Form 5-10 (continued)

LOCATION OF ASSETS AND DOCUMENTS

1. Safe Deposit Box:
   Location and Number _____
   Who Has Access _____
   Who Has Keys _____

2. Original, Current Wills _____

3. Life, Health, and Accident Insurance Policies:
   a. _____
   b. _____
   c. _____
   d. _____

4. Passbooks (Where Kept):
   a. _____
   b. _____

5. Securities:
   a. _____
   b. _____
   c. _____

6. Trust Agreements:

7. Tax Returns, Years Covered:

8. Contract and Business Agreements:

9. Real Estate and Condominiums:
   a. Location and How Owned _____
   b. Deed and Title Policy _____
   c. Mortgages and Insurance _____
   d. Leases _____

10. Custodial and Other Managed Accounts:

11. Jewelry and Other Valuables:

12. Canceled Checks and Stubs, Period Covered:

ROLE, TASKS, AND OBLIGATIONS

Form 5-10 (continued)

13. Cemetery Plot(s), Location, Deed, and Care Arrangements:
    a. _____
    b. _____

14. Birth Certificates:
    a. _____
    b. _____

15. Marriage Certificates:
    Pre- and Post Nuptial Agreements:

16. Divorce Papers:

17. Employee Benefits Statements:

18. Employee and Government Benefit Plan Copies:

19. Military Discharge Papers:

20. Naturalization Papers:

21. Passports:

22. Adoption Papers:

23. General Insurance Policies:
    a. _____
    b. _____
    c. _____

24. Private Safe, Location, and Who Has Access:

25. Firearms and Registrations:
    a. _____
    b. _____
    c. _____

26. Funeral Directions:

27. Powers of Attorney Outstanding, Including Bank Accounts and Safe Deposit Access: (Give dates and names, show attorney in fact, address, and description of power):

28. Living Wills or Directives to Physicians:

CHAPTER 5

Official Forms

Contact your registry of wills, probate office, or related entity, requesting all official forms necessary for probate. Make a list by name and number.

NAME OF OFFICE   PHONE NUMBER

_____

_____

_____

_____

_____

Business Law

Paralegals are instrumental players in many business establishments, whether sole proprietorships or corporations.

Reserve a Corporate Name

Respond to the following questions:

Agency Charged with Corporate Name Registration

Telephone

Policy for Corporate Name Reservation

Cost

Filing Requirements

Forms (Specify and Attach)

Partnerships

Respond to these questions regarding partnerships in your jurisdiction:

Statutory Controls

Filing Requirements

Costs for Filing on Maintenance

Forms (Specify and Attach)

ROLE, TASKS, AND OBLIGATIONS

Conduct a corporate dissolution interview using the checklist in Form 5-11.

Form 5-11[7]

Intern Name_____Date_____

Corporate Dissolution Checklist

1. Obtain a resolution to dissolve the corporation from stockholders.
2. Prepare federal IRS Form 966, *Corporate Dissolution or Liquidation*.
3. Request final statements from all creditors and pay them.
4. Pay all applicable taxes and obtain receipts.
5. Prepare and file a certificate of dissolution with the Secretary of State.
6. Notify the Workers' Compensation Department in your state; file applicable papers.
7. File IRS Form 940, *Employer's Annual Federal Unemployment Tax Return*.
8. File *a Report of Employer on Disposition of Business in Whole or in Part* with the state unemployment department.
9. Notify the Social Security Department. File IRS Form W-3, *Transmittal of Income and Tax Statements* and IRS Form W-2.
10. Notify the Sales Tax Commission; file a final sales tax report.
11. Publish a notice in local paper.
12. Determine the amount of liquidated dividends and when they can be paid.
13. File IRS Forms 1096 and 1099-DIV.
14. File a Federal Income Tax return, IRS Form 1120.
15. Explore the possibility of investment credit recapture of IRS § 38 property.
16. Investigate the depreciation recapture on real estate.
17. Prepare a claim for refund, if applicable.
18. Arrange for storage of records.
19. Notify utilities regarding the cancellation of services.
20. Notify insurance agents regarding policy cancellation or revision.
21. Cancel outstanding stock certificates.
22. Explore the possibility of being classified as a Collapsible Corporation.
23. Determine whether there is a possibility the corporation will become a personal holding company.
24. Determine and pay special taxes.
25. Determine the effect of liquidating gains and losses on stockholders.

Civil Practice

No paralegal will practice long without confronting the rigors of civil practice. This practice area varies from negligence to product liability, from defamation to wrongful termination.

CHAPTER 5

*Reproduction
of the Accident
Scene*

Make a chart or illustration that portrays the accident scene using the template below.

Prepare a chart or illustration that portrays the scene of an accident.

Key

N
W — E
S

ROLE, TASKS, AND OBLIGATIONS

Produce a series of photographs of the auto accident making use of the checklist at Form 5-12.

Form 5-12[8]

Intern Name_____Date_____

Photography Checklist

What to Photograph:

1. Vehicle Identification
    a. Vehicle license plate
    b. Vehicle identification plate
    c. Vehicle's make and model
2. Contact damage area
    a. Overlap
    b. Collapse
    c. Direction of thrust
3. Induced damage area
4. Undamaged area
5. Interior — when needed
6. Vehicle lamps
7. Vehicle tires
8. Close-up photographs

Plaintiff's Damages

Calculate the plaintiff's damages under the following categories:

Vehicle Collision Costs $ _____
Repairs $ _____
Towing $ _____
Personal Property $ _____
Economic Losses $ _____
Lost Wages $ _____
Pain and Suffering $ _____
Medical Costs $ _____
Emergency $ _____

Total $ _____

CHAPTER 5

Product
Liability

Arrange for a deposition in a case of product liability.

Contact:
    Opposing Counsel
    Expert Witnesses
    Responsible Attorney
    Videotape Operator.

Prepare Notice of Depositions (if applicable).

Summarize proceedings on a deposition index similar to the one in Form 5-13.

Form 5-13[9]

Intern Name_____Date_____

Deposition Index

PAGE	LINE	SUMMARY
8	7	Doe purchased the coffeemaker in question on July 2, 1994.
8	11	The coffee pot worked properly for two weeks.
8	20	Doe followed the directions and used the coffeemaker properly every time.
9	2	Doe had the coffeemaker plugged into a grounded outlet.
9	17	On July 17, 1994, Doe noticed a strange smell when the coffeemaker was turned on.
10	22	Doe cleaned the coffeemaker according to the manufacturer's directions.
12	6	When Doe turned the coffeemaker on to proceed with the cleaning, the coffeemaker made a loud popping noise and caught on fire.
12	12	The fire that resulted damaged one wall of the kitchen.
12	20	The fire company was called to extinguish the fire, and the entire kitchen suffered water damage as a result.

Upon receipt of transcription, create a log according to Form 5-14.

ROLE, TASKS, AND OBLIGATIONS

Form 5-14[10]

Intern Name_____Date_____

Deposition Log

Deponent	Date	Documents Prepared	Volume/ Pages	Exhibit Numbers	Attorney/ Paralegal	Notes and Comments

Case Number_____

Case Name_____

Legend:
N/N--not necessary
S/B--separate binder (exhibits)
N/A--not attached (exhibits)

CHAPTER 5

Witness Testimony

At a trial, track or outline witness testimony according to Form 5-15.

Form 5-15

Intern Name_____Date_____

Outline of Witness Testimony

Name of Client _____	
Name of Witness _____	

Notes on Testimony	Notes for Cross-Examination

ROLE, TASKS, AND OBLIGATIONS

List all exhibits for an upcoming trial in Form 5-16.

Form 5-16

Intern Name_____Date_____

List of Exhibits

Plaintiff's Exhibits			
Name of Client _____			
Offer	**Rec'd**	**No.**	**Description**

CHAPTER 5

Emotional
Distress

In a case of intentional infliction of emotional distress, the plaintiff may allege sexual harassment. Conduct a client consultation using Form 5-17.

Form 5-17[11]

Intern Name_____Date_____

Sexual Harassment Complaint

(1) Date Report Received _____

(2) Please provide the following information about (the person filing the report with you).
Gender: male _____ female _____
Department or administrative unit (if appropriate) _____

(3) Please provide the following information about _____ (the person about whom the report is filed).
Gender: male _____ female _____
Department or administrative unit (if appropriate) _____

(4) Date(s) of reported incident(s)._____
Where did the reported incident(s) occur? _____

(5) Briefly describe the incident(s) as reported. _____
_____
_____

(6) Categorize the incident(s) being reported (check all that apply).
sexist comments _____
sexual comments_____
undue attention _____
invitations _____
physical advances_____
sexual propositions_____
sexual bribery_____
other _____

(7) What action was requested by the person filing the report with you? _____
_____

(8) What action did you take in response to the information reported to you? _____
_____

(continued)

ROLE, TASKS, AND OBLIGATIONS

Form 5–17 (continued)

(9) Should further involvement by the Affirmative Action Office be initiated? Yes _____ No_____

(10) Feel free to provide additional comments on the back of this form.

    Person receiving the report:
        Name _____
        Department _____
        Signature _____ Date _____

Questions about completing this summary should be directed to the Assistant Affirmative Action Officer. Upon completion, return this form (labeled confidential) to him or her.

Legal Research

Conduct an inventory of your sponsor's legal collection in a format similar to Form 5-18. Be aware that all or part of the collection could be in CD-ROM format.

Form 5–18

Law Library

Resource	Inventory
Encyclopedia	List:
State/Federal Court Reports	List:
State Statutes	List States:
Treatises and Formbooks	List Title and Topic:
Practice Series	List Title and Topic:

CHAPTER 5

Computerized Legal Services

If your sponsor has computerized legal research services, find the following information:

Name of service
Capacity
Types of courts accessible
List five courts.

Ability to update, amend or supplement cases? Yes _____ No _____

Administrative Law

In many cases the right to advocate in administrative proceedings is extended to paralegals.

Federal Agencies

Create a chart or database of all federal agencies located in your jurisdiction. Some examples follow.

National Labor Relations Board
Address:_____
_____
Phone:_____

Department of Justice
Address:_____
_____
Phone:_____

Department of Defense
Address:_____
_____
Phone:_____

Department of Immigration and Naturalization
Address:_____
_____
Phone:_____

Department of Interior
Address:_____
_____
Phone:_____

Now that you understand your role as an intern, it is time to evaluate the site of your internship.

ROLE, TASKS, AND OBLIGATIONS

Endnotes

1. Lawrence A. Tower, Automobile Warranty Litigation, *39 American Jury Trials* 28-30 (1989).
2. Edward E. Bates, Jr., *Georgia Domestic Relations Forms: Practice* 560-562 Reprinted with permission of Michie Butterworth, 1991.
3. Charles P. Nemeth, *Real Estate for the Pennsylvania Paralegal* (manuscript Chapter 2 at 49-53, on file with author). Copyright 1995, George T. Bisel Co., Philadelphia, PA 1/800-247-3526.
4. Charles P. Nemeth, *Real Estate for the Pennsylvania Paralegal* (manuscript Chapter 2 at 54-56, on file with author). Copyright 1995, George T. Bisel Co., Philadelphia, PA 1/800-247-3526.
5. See 7 Federal Procedural Forms at Form 20:30.
6. For an excellent practice series, see Research Institute of America, *Estate Planning and Coordination* (1989).
7. James A. Douglas and Patrick Hamill, *Modern Corporation Checklists* 20-14/20-17, 3d ed. (1990), Warren, Gorham, & Lamont, Inc., Boston.
8. Northwestern University Traffic Institute, *Vehicle Damage Photography* 2-3 "SN7717."
9. Dianne D. Zalewski and Joyce Walden, *Paralegal Discovery: Organization and Management* 2-11, Wiley Law Publications (1991).
10. Dianne D. Zalewski and Joyce Walden, *Paralegal Discovery: Organization and Management* 2-12, Wiley Law Publications (1991).
11. Charles P. Nemeth, *Business Forms for the Paralegal*, John Wiley and Sons, (1995)

CHAPTER 5

CHAPTER 6
THE INTERNSHIP SITE

A focused examination of the internship site will greatly assist you as you perform the activities of your internship. What is the nature and organization of the internship location? What formal methods of management exist within the location? What lines of authority exist? Are there informal means of operation? Who really has the power in the office? What are the goals and purposes of the organization? How is labor delegated and differentiated? In short, get to know the ins and outs, all the nooks and crannies of the place that will be your temporary professional home. It is best to specify precisely what is expected of your sponsor. Evaluate Figure 6-1, a series of sponsor tasks and functions.

Figure 6-1[1]

Responsibilities of the Sponsor

1. The sponsor is responsible for accepting a student to perform an internship under his or her supervision.

2. The sponsor must ensure that the internship enables the student to gain meaningful law-related knowledge and exposure. The internship must be appropriate for local law practice. The task or series of tasks must require at least _____ hours to complete.

3. The sponsor must sign the Internship Authorization Form.

4. The sponsor must ensure that sufficient equipment and/or materials are available to carry out the assigned tasks.

5. For each stage of the internship, some initial explanation or directions should be provided. The sponsor must establish a timetable for completing various tasks.

6. The sponsor must hold a conference with the student regularly during the course of the internship. Conferences must be scheduled at regular intervals, such as when the student completes _____ hours, _____ hours, _____ hours, _____ hours, and after completion of the internship. The sponsor must specify the goals and tasks to be accomplished prior to each conference. During these conferences the student will report on his or her progress to date. The sponsor will review and sign the Daily Log, evaluate the student's progress, and provide additional instruction and direction. The sponsor should also discuss specific plans to enable the student to progress further.

7. The sponsor must complete the Sponsor's Evaluation Form upon the student's completion of the internship. The sponsor must review the Evaluation with the student and ask the student to sign it. The sponsor must return the Evaluation Form to the internship coordinator.

CHAPTER 6

8. The sponsor is not required to pay the student for this learning experience. However, the sponsor is expected to reimburse the student for any expenses incurred while performing work for the office.

9. Sponsors are invited to assign the student a special project within the law firm. This project must be suitable for a legal assistant. The sponsor may also require the student to complete a research project or series of projects on a particular area of law or procedure. Some suggested topics include the following:

    a. Chapter 7 bankruptcy procedures
    b. Methods of preparing a witness for deposition
    c. Flow charts and checklists for doing legal research
    d. Methods for handling adoptions
    e. Fact investigation in debt collection cases
    f. Law firm marketing
    g. Procedures for drafting interrogatories
    h. Procedures for preparing for trials and hearings
    i. Research and analysis of public records and hearings
    j. Docket and calendar control systems for the law office
    k. Comparison of roles of litigation paralegals in various size law firms
    l. Procedures for handling and maintaining client files and records.

Interns could also be given a checklist of functions with a simultaneous timeline to follow. See Figure 6-2.

Figure 6-2

Functions of the Intern

MINIMAL INTERN ACTIVITIES OVER A 200- TO 300-HOUR COURSE

Check, Shepardize, and "bluebook" citations. **3-5 hours**
Proof. **1 hour**
Draft simple pleadings. **3-5 hours**
Draft facts sections of some briefs and memoranda. **3-5 hours**
Supervise mechanical production and distribution. **1 hour**
Assist in organizing and conducting file searches. **2 hours**
Digest, abstract, and index documents. **3-5 hours**
Develop a retrieval system. **1-3 hours**
Draft factual memoranda based on data contained in documents. **1-3 hours**
Digest and index deposition transcripts. **3-5 hours**
Prepare materials to brief witnesses before deposition hearings. **3-5 hours**
Assist in briefing witnesses. **1-3 hours**
Organize and analyze answers to interrogatories. **3-5 hours**
Draft simple interrogatories and answers. **3-5 hours**

THE INTERNSHIP SITE

Figure 6-2 (continued)

Assemble factual data used in preparing and answering interrogatories. **3-5 hours**
Gather and organize factual material for trials. **3-5 hours**
Develop charts, graphs, and other visual aids. **4-6 hours**
Take notes and handle exhibits at trials. **1-3 hours**
Assemble rebuttal evidence. **1 hour**
Digest and index transcripts. **3-5 hours**
Prepare preliminary drafts of wills and trusts from sample forms. **3-5 hours**
Obtain information from court records. **4-6 hours**
Research and analyze public records. **4-6 hours**
Attend and report on legislative and administrative hearings. **7-8 hours**
Compile legislative histories. **3-5 hours**
Maintain a master docket calendar. **1-3 hours**
Assist in administration of the law library. **4-6 hours**

The Internship Supervisor/ Sponsor

The sponsoring entity will assign you an immediate supervisor. This person will play an important role in your internship. Your supervisor should have a sincere interest in you, be available for consultation, provide guidance and insight, and lay out a master plan for you to follow. An uninterested person who grudgingly takes on a supervisory role can destroy the positive nature of an internship. There's no harm in doing a bit of research into the personalities of the people at the sponsoring firm. You may be able to request a supervisor who is not only experienced and willing to take on the responsibility of an intern, but who also possesses the interpersonal skills to make you feel at home.

Interaction With Internship or Placement Coordinator

If your educational institution has an internship program, there will be an internship coordinator or placement director working to create relationships with sponsoring firms. Those entrusted with establishing internships must lay out just what is expected of both interns and sponsors. You can review the series of responsibilities typically assigned to the placement director or internship coordinator at Figure 6-3.

CHAPTER 6

Figure 6-3[2]

Responsibilities of the Internship Overseer

PLACEMENT DIRECTOR OR INTERNSHIP
COORDINATOR'S RESPONSIBILITIES

1. The placement director (with any necessary support staff) is charged with facilitating successful completion of the internships.

2. The placement director or internship coordinator conducts an internship orientation to assist students in making the most of their internships. The following topics are discussed:

   a. Practical aspects of working in a law office, including: legal ethics, office procedure, professionalism, time management, confidentiality, court procedure and decorum, office politics, and the role of legal assistants in specific substantive areas.

   b. Guidelines for securing an internship. Students are instructed that they are responsible for soliciting their own placement and that all internships must be approved by the placement director or internship coordinator before the student begins work.

3. The coordinator works with potential sponsors to develop appropriate internship opportunities. One of the placement director's goals is to nurture long-term relationships with sponsors in order to benefit the needs of many students.

4. The coordinator screens potential candidates for sponsors and forwards to the sponsor the resumes of those who fit the sponsor's needs.

5. The coordinator serves as an advisor for students during selection and completion of the internship.

6. The coordinator evaluates the student's proposed internship in order to ensure that the institute's requirements are satisfied.

7. The coordinator contacts the sponsor before the internship begins to reiterate the sponsor's responsibilities.

8. The coordinator contacts the sponsor during the internship to monitor the progress of the internship and to ensure that the student is being supervised.

9. The coordinator contacts the student during the internship to monitor the progress of the internship and to ensure that the student is receiving appropriate supervision.

10. The coordinator contacts the sponsor after the student has completed the internship to thank him or her for participating and to remind him or her to complete and return the Sponsor's Evaluation Form.

11. The coordinator conveys feedback regarding the quality and relevance of the curricula to the appropriate academic officers.

THE INTERNSHIP SITE

Sponsors and Interns

The manner in which you interact with your sponsor is often a matter of personality and preference. At first, you will rely heavily on your sponsor's insight and guidance. As time progresses and you gain confidence, you will act more independently. Even so, regular meetings or visitations between intern and supervisor are essential to an internship.

The supervision schedule you set up with your supervisor will depend on whether or not you work together on a daily basis. If you work with your supervisor daily, the tendency is to discuss issues, problems, and questions as they arise. This type of supervision has some shortcomings, however, if more formal meetings are not scheduled. You may find that after rethinking and researching an issue, and/or discussing it with a fellow intern or agency employee, you have new ideas or questions about it that you would like to discuss with your supervisor. Without a scheduled session, this may be difficult to fit into a daily routine.[3]

The supervisor may wish to formalize the visitation as follows in Form 6-1.

Form 6-1

Intern Name_____Date_____

Supervisor/Sponsor Visitation

Intern:	Meeting Date:	Length of Meeting:
Subjects Discussed:		
Signature of Intern:	Signature of Supervisor/Sponsor:	

CHAPTER 6

These meetings should spotlight both progress and problems. If you are in need of specific recommendations for improvement, your sponsor should note this in a progress report like Form 6-2.

Form 6-2

Intern Name_____Date_____

Progress Report

To:
From:
Progress Notes
Problem Areas
Recommended Change
Signature of Supervisor/Sponsor

THE INTERNSHIP SITE

Your sponsor may also wish to chart meetings, consultations, and observation periods on Form 6-3.

Form 6-3

Intern Name_____Date_____

Consultation/Observation Charts

Intern:		Sponsor:
I. Consultation		
Date	Topics	
II. Observation		
Date	Intern Activity	

153

CHAPTER 6

How heavily the educational institution weighs the recommendations of the sponsor is a question of policy. Most institutions and their faculty supervisors afford a great deal of credibility to the sponsors' views because of their unique and intimate opportunity to observe the paralegal intern in action. Full coverage of evaluation techniques and various instruments for conducting the evaluation are found in Chapter Seven.

Finally, paralegal interns should be asked to evaluate the performance of their sponsors. The internship coordinator or faculty supervisor will use their evaluation to assist in future internship placements. See Form 6-4.

Form 6–4

Intern Name_____Date_____

Student Evaluation of the Internship Sponsor

Name of Supervisor
Punctuality
Ability to Listen
Guidance
Explanation of Policies
Availability
Comments

154

THE INTERNSHIP
SITE

Faculty Supervision

Since some institutions provide the intern with faculty supervision, some discussion of the supervisor's function is warranted.

First and foremost, the faculty supervisor serves as a liaison between the internship site and the educational institution. As a result, various correspondence is necessary between the parties, namely the sponsor and the institution. A letter of introduction should announce the faculty supervisor to the sponsor. See Figure 6-4.

Figure 6-4

Letter of Introduction

_____[Sponsor's name]
_____[Address]
_____[City, State, Zip]

Dear _____,

Thank you so much for agreeing to sponsor [Name of Student Intern] as an intern in your firm/agency/company. Your interest in our Internship Program is greatly appreciated.

I will be [Name of Student Intern]'s faculty advisor for his/her internship in the upcoming semester. If you have any questions regarding the program's policies or procedures, do not hesitate to call me. I have enclosed an Internship Program Package that includes all information that is necessary for you as a sponsor.

I will be making periodic visits to the internship site to monitor the intern's on-the-job performance. I will, of course, schedule these visits at a time convenient for both of us. I also like to meet with the sponsor at the middle and end of the semester to sit down and discuss the intern's progress. This helps to uncover any performance areas the interns may find difficult, and enables us to exchange ideas on ways they may improve their performance.

Thank you again for your interest in our Internship Program. Please feel free to call me anytime.

With warm regards,

Faculty Advisor

155

CHAPTER 6

Second, it is advisable to send a memo requesting a progress report on the intern's activity midway through the internship. See Figure 6-5.

Figure 6-5

Request for Midterm Progress Report

MEMO

TO: All Internship Sponsors
FROM: Internship Faculty Advisors
DATE:
RE: Midsemester Internship Evaluation

Please remember to forward your midsemester evaluations to your intern's faculty advisor no later than
_____ , 19 __ .
Please use the evaluation form included in the Internship Program Package. Thank you for your cooperation and continued support!

Third, a letter requesting all final evaluations and related documentation from the sponsor is a good strategy and assures timely submission. See Figure 6-6.

Figure 6-6

Request for Final Evaluation

_____ ,19_____
_____[Sponsor's name]
_____[Address]
_____[City, State, Zip]

RE: Final Internship Evaluation of: [Intern's Name]

Dear _____ ,

It is time to submit your final evaluation of the paralegal interns you are supervising. Please review the semester's assignments and work experience with your interns. This evaluation should be an opportunity to provide the students with valuable, constructive criticism about their semester's performance. Please use the form included in the Internship Program Package you received earlier this year.

THE INTERNSHIP
SITE

Figure 6-6 (continued)

This evaluation, along with the student's daily log, seminar attendance, samples of work, and final report, will give us the information necessary to determine if the student has fulfilled the requirements of the Internship Program for credit.

Please be sure to complete the evaluation and submit it by _____ , 19_____ . If you have any questions please contact me.

Thank you for participating in the Paralegal Internship Program this semester. I hope the experience has been enjoyable and of mutual benefit for you and your staff and that you will continue to participate in our program.

With warm regards,

Faculty Advisor

Faculty supervisors are usually entrusted not only with the collection of reports and documentation, but also with their review and evaluation for grading purposes. Faculty supervisors will also correspond with interns, advising them of their current status. See Figure 6-7.

Figure 6-7

Status Advisory

Dear John,

This note reviews your performance to date.

Hours Performed as of _____ , 19 _____ .
Intern Diaries Submitted as of _____, 19 _____ .
Midterm Sponsor Evaluation. Received _____ Not Received _____
Research Papers: Date Received
      Number 1 _____
      Number 2 _____
      Number 3 _____

I'll keep you posted periodically. I hope everything is going well.

With best regards,

Faculty Supervisor/Internship Coordinator

CHAPTER 6

At the end of the internship, the faculty supervisor should tabulate all grades and assignments in a central database like Figure 6-8.

Figure 6-8

Grade/Assignment Database

Name of Intern:	Name of Faculty Supervisor:	
1. Sponsor Evaluation		
2. Faculty Supervisor Evaluation		
3. Diary or Log		
4. Research Papers		
5. Other Assignments		
	Final Grade	

The Sponsoring Organization

Learning about the design and operation your sponsoring organization will help you meet designated standards. Your performance is not solely measured by your individual proficiency, but gauged as to sponsor fit, seeing whether or not you meld into the agency or firm and act in accordance with agency or firm philosophy. Sometimes the most technically competent person may be unable to adjust to a particular workplace. This section is designed to help you understand the site you have chosen.

The Paralegal's Place in the Sponsoring Organization

As a paralegal, you are considered support personnel. Your position exists because of an attorney, and primary oversight of your work rests with the supervising attorney. Because avoiding unauthorized practice of law naturally depends on supervision, it is crucial that you know your function. The novice paralegal can fall into many traps. What to do and what not to do are unceasing concerns.

158

THE INTERNSHIP SITE

As long as you understand your position, problems can be avoided. The American Bar Association's definition of a paralegal or legal assistant refers to this alliance between lawyers and paralegals:

> A legal assistant is a person, qualified through education, training, or work experience, who is employed or retained by a lawyer, law office, governmental agency, or other entity in a capacity or function which involves the performance, under the ultimate direction and supervision of an attorney, of specifically delegated substantive legal work, which work, for the most part, requires a sufficient knowledge of legal concepts that, absent such assistant, the attorney would perform the task.

The National Federation of Paralegal Associations confirms this philosophy of the occupational role:

> A paralegal/legal assistant is a person qualified through education, training or work experience to perform substantive legal work that requires knowledge of legal concepts that is customarily, but not exclusively, performed by a lawyer. This person may be retained or employed by a lawyer, law office, governmental agency, or other entity or may be authorized by administrative, statutory or court authority to perform this work.

The National Association of Legal Assistants follows the same path:

> The terms being used interchangeably to identify these individuals are: legal assistant, paralegal, free-lance legal assistant, independent paralegal and legal technician. Each refers to non-lawyers engaged in a career related to legal services. The important distinction among these terms is how those legal services are delivered.[4]

To further understand your role, look at existing job descriptions prepared by the sponsor. A job description outlines those functions delegated to paralegals, the competencies required, and those tasks properly within a paralegal's parameters. Armed with a job description, you will begin your internship knowing the territory to master. In the absence of a job description, ask your supervisor to write, possibly in memorandum form, the tasks appropriately assigned to the paralegal intern.

CHAPTER 6

Organization, Decision Making, and Structure of the Internship Site

Understanding the administrative hierarchy of your sponsoring agency will enhance your performance as an intern. Knowing where you fit in the scheme of organizational design gives you a sense of purpose. For example, for what department or legal specialty in the firm will you be working? Who is your direct supervisor? What are the policies of the office? What are the goals and purposes of the agency?

Who runs the show and how things get done are crucial concerns for the paralegals. How does an organizational flow chart unfold? Look at a simple example of a company below:

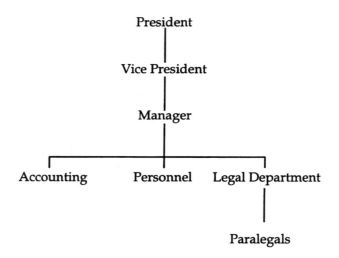

A small business might operate in this fashion: a hierarchy of people with the buck stopping at the president's door. Some law firms have sophisticated operational designs. How does one differentiate senior from junior partners? How does one become a partner? What makes a lawyer an employee, not a partner? Who is a lawyer designated "of counsel"? Do lawyers supervise one another? Consider the chart in Figure 6-9 on the following page, when composing your own internship graphics. For more information about law office structure, read *Law Office Dynamics* by Charlotte W. Smith, Esq., published by Pearson Publications Company, Dallas, TX.

THE INTERNSHIP SITE

Figure 6-9

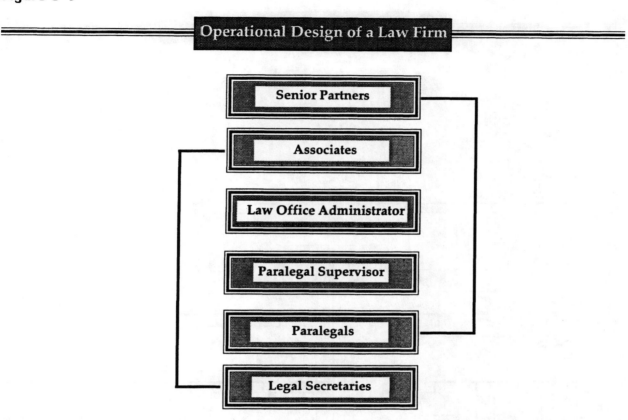

Of course, this is merely one formal model of decision making. Assume you are interning for the U.S. Attorney's Office, part of the U.S. Justice Department. How do the lines of authority run? Who makes decisions? How many departments or divisions are there? Look at the chart in Figure 6-10 for the Justice Department's hierarchy.

CHAPTER 6

Figure 6-10

Hierarchy of the Department of Justice

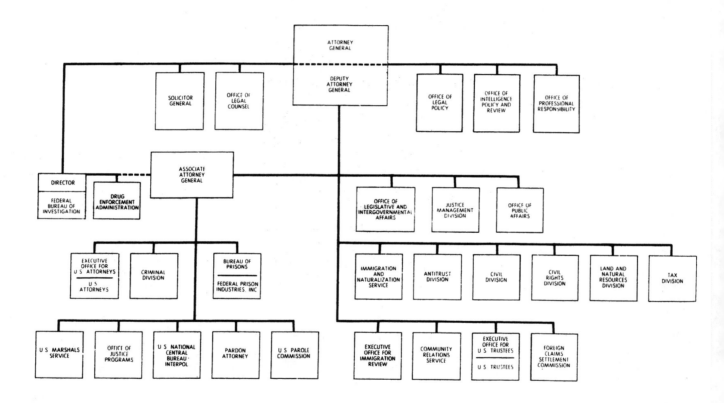

THE INTERNSHIP SITE

These departments, divisions, and offices represent specific purposes assigned to select individuals. The paralegal intern will fit in somewhere. The intern cannot simply say, "I intern at the U.S. Department of Justice." The comment is so broad, so unfocused, that the intern really knows little or nothing of what all the internship will entail. To know that, the intern must focus narrowly, raising questions like

What Division of the U.S. Department of Justice?
What unit of that division?
What task force of that unit?
What title or role will the intern play?
Who is my immediate supervisor?
Who is my supervisor's supervisor?
What are the goals and purposes of my assigned location?
What is my job title and job description?

Use the schematic in Form 6-5, or alter it if necessary, to chart and portray your location's bureaucratic, hierarchical design.

Form 6-5

Intern Name_____Date_____

Hierarchy of Internship Site

CHAPTER 6

Those interning in government agencies will soon discern the multiple levels of operation and the mind-boggling tiers of oversight. It is more difficult to find your place and purpose here than in most other internship experiences. Take a look at Figure 6-11, a pictorial representation of the Veterans Administration. Try your own agency's structure, using the Veterans Administration as a model.

Figure 6-11

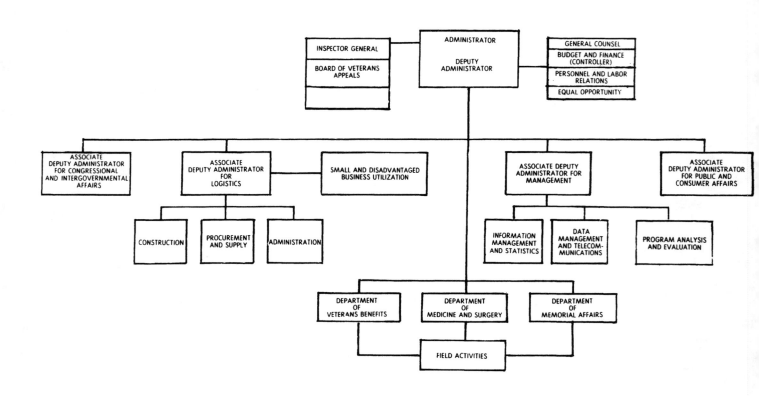

Structure of the Veterans Administration

THE INTERNSHIP SITE

Informal Structure and Operation of the Internship Site

Now that you have studied the preceding organization charts, consider your sponsoring agency in action.

1. Compare and contrast the powers and authority granted your office with powers actually exercised. If not exercised, who takes over the responsibilities?
2. What office has a reputation for efficiency and poor performance? Do the employees adhere to job titles?
3. What office has a reputation for inefficiency and solid performance? What jobs have a reputation for not getting done?
4. Name officers (if applicable) who appear to delegate their authority widely.
5. Name supervising attorneys (if applicable) who do not supervise at all and tend to delegate liberally to interns.
6. Are there nonprofessional employees who tend to wield enormous power? If yes, what are their positions?
7. Are the policies and procedures of the company, law firm, or agency uniformly applied? If no, explain how.
8. Are there circumstances in the law firm, company, or agency, where a subordinate tells a superior what to do? If yes, explain.
9. Have you witnessed paralegals actually practicing law, giving legal advice, and acting in an unauthorized manner? If yes, explain.

Budgetary Concerns of the Internship Site

Much can be learned about an agency, firm, or company by its reserves and expenditures. Budgets reveal where the action is in the law firm, how healthy the profits are in the business, and where legislative priorities are for the agency.

The primary instrument of fiscal planning is the budget. A budget details how the company or agency will be run by projecting income and expenditures. By analyzing past, present, and future expenses, a company can project, with reasonable reliability, its financial future. Fiscal planning should be an ongoing activity. A budget is not a tool to be constructed and put aside; it is a tool that should be used on a daily basis.

Sizeable increases or decreases in budgetary figures often imply profitability or financial difficulty. Most budgets are divided into two categories: **operating capital/income** and **expenses/liabilities**. In the case of a law firm, billable hours serve as the income source, with a series of expenses drawn against it, as shown in Form 6-6.

By analyzing budgets, one can see where the money comes from and where it goes.

165

CHAPTER 6

Form 6-6

Intern Name_____Date_____

Capital/Income and Expense/Liability Chart

Income	
Dividends	
Expenses	
Wages	
Withholding Tax	
Dividends	
Office Rent	
Supplies	
Fees	
Professional Expenses	
Utilities	
Consulting	
Advertising	
Travel and Food	
Total	

THE INTERNSHIP SITE

Conclusion

In government agencies, political influences have an impact on budgets. Criminal justice agencies are often influenced by the political clamor about drugs, investigation, and prisons. As the noise increases, budgets usually escalate. When silence returns, the budget abates. All this being true, budgets tell us something about whom the intern serves.

Gaining access to budgetary information is generally easy in public companies and agencies of government. It is difficult to get in law firms, and as an intern you are better off not asking for it.

Endnotes

1. American Institute for Paralegal Studies, Inc., Southfield, MI 48075.
2. American Institute for Paralegal Studies, Inc., Southfield, MI 48075.
3. Gary R. Gordon and R. Bruce McBride, *Criminal Justice Internships* 2d ed., 50 (1991), Anderson Pub. Co.
4. National Association of Legal Assistants, Inc., Connie Kretchmer, *The Issues: What Are They? Who Are They Talking About?* (1991).

CHAPTER 6

CHAPTER 7

EVALUATING THE INTERN EXPERIENCE

When you reach the evaluation stage, your internship sojourn is almost over. Now you will assess and weigh your experience, its players, and the activities in which you engaged. You, of course, are the center of this examination. By enrolling in this course, you have chosen to be judged on performance, to be graded and evaluated by others. You will also be asked to evaluate the level of the supervision you received. Sponsors or supervisors make an indelible impression on interns, and their mark must be meaningful. Finally, the internship site, whether law firm, business, or government agency, is worthy of your scrutiny. The fundamental question is whether the internship site is of benefit to future students.

The manner in which these final evaluations unfold is hard to predict. Much depends on your original expectations, whether realistic or not, and the sponsor's ability to meet them. In the legal scenario, interns often have grandiose views of what they will do. A paralegal interning at a litigation firm cannot expect to argue cases but will only observe proceedings. Student internship judgments must be examined in a practical context, in light of what can and cannot be done. Following is a review of these evaluation practices and their corresponding forms.

Student Evaluation of the Internship

How interns and their sponsors perceive the internship experience is a formidable policy concern for both the educational institutions and the agencies or firms participating in the program. Satisfaction rates tell sponsoring institutions whether the relationship should continue.

The Student Description and Evaluation of Internship Program in Form 7-1 fully encapsulates the student's assessment. Interns are asked a series of questions involving the following:

> personal development
> professional development
> strengths and weaknesses of the experience
> placement potential
> correlation between learning objectives and actual results.

CHAPTER 7

Form 7-1

Intern Name_____Date_____

Student Description and Evaluation of Internship Program

The information requested below will provide valuable information relating to the Internship Project. Complete the form in detail with responsible answers.

Please PRINT Clearly or Type the Appropriate Responses.

Name _____ Date _____

Major _____ Year _____

Agency_____

Location _____

Supervisor activity _____

Your assignment or work area _____

What are your normal assignment week's hours? _____

Describe in detail your assignment with this firm:

    1. Was the placement meaningful to your personal development?
    2. Was the placement meaningful to your professional development?
    3. What do you consider the best feature of this placement?
    4. What do you consider the weak points of this placement?
    5. To what extent did your supervisor affect your evaluation of this placement?
    6. Was training or orientation available?
    7. Does this firm offer potential for after-graduation employment?
    8. What is the likelihood that, if offered, you would accept a permanent position with this firm?
    9. Do you feel that the in-service learning objectives were realistic and valid?

Remarks (if any)

Intern's Signature _____ Date _____

EVALUATING
THE INTERNSHIP EXPERIENCE

Form 7-2[1]

Another evaluation mechanism, the Post-Internship Evaluation, is reproduced at Form 7-2. At the end, the survey properly asks the intern for suggestions on how to improve the internship offerings.

Post-Internship Evaluation

Student Name_____ Date_____

Sponsor's Name and Address

_____

_____

1. Were you given adequate supervision by your sponsor?
   Yes _____   No _____
2. Was your internship supervisor actively involved in your learning activities? Please describe.
3. Were you assigned meaningful tasks?
   Yes _____   No _____
4. What type of training was available? Please describe.
   Formal _____ Informal _____ Both _____
5. Are you working for your internship sponsor?
   Yes_____   No _____ (If No, skip to question 9.)
6. If you are working for your internship sponsor, what is your employment status?
   Full Time ____ Part Time_____ What is your job title? _____
7. Have you been offered a permanent position with your internship sponsor?
   Yes _____   No _____
8. If you were offered permanent employment, did you accept?
   Yes _____   No _____
9. If you are not presently working for your internship sponsor, which of the following is applicable?
   ☐ My services were terminated upon completion of the internship period by the sponsor.
   ☐ I was asked to continue on the job by my internship sponsor, but I did not choose to do so.
   ☐ Other. Please explain.
10. If you have accepted permanent employment with your sponsor, what is your salary?
    _____per hour (or) _____ per week (or) _____ per year
11. Would you give your permission for any of the above data to be used in a recruiting situation?
    Yes_____   No _____
12. How would you rate the overall effectiveness of the internship?
13. What suggestions would you make for improving the internship program?

Thank you for taking the time to complete this evaluation. We sincerely hope that you have had a valuable and worthwhile internship experience. Best wishes for much continued success in all you do!

Intern's Signature _____ Date _____

CHAPTER 7

In this format, the student intern covers similar territory involving the pros and the cons of the internship experience. However, the survey emphasizes the connection between the internship and future job placement by asking questions about

place of employment
level of compensation
job title
whether internship became an actual job.

Some institutions utilize more than one student evaluation mechanism. In some cases, during the actual internship, students are asked to complete a midterm, or halfway-point evaluation like Form 7-3.

Form 7-3

Midterm Evaluation

Student Name_____ Date _____
Sponsor's Name and Address

_____
_____
_____

1. Are you being given adequate supervision by your sponsor?
   Yes _____   No _____
2. Is your internship supervisor actively involved in your learning activities? Please describe.
3. Are you being assigned meaningful tasks?
   Yes _____   No _____
4. What type of training is available? Please describe.
   Formal _____ Informal _____ Both _____
5. Have you discussed permanent employment opportunities with your internship sponsor?
   Yes _____   No _____
6. If you have discussed employment opportunities, has an offer been made?
   Yes _____   No _____
7. Discuss this issue of paralegal employment and internship benefits with your sponsor. What comments does your sponsor provide?
8. At this point, how would you rate the overall effectiveness of the internship?

Thank you for taking the time to complete this evaluation. We sincerely hope that you are having a valuable and worthwhile internship experience. Best wishes for continued success as you proceed.

EVALUATING
THE INTERNSHIP EXPERIENCE

This midterm activity evaluation prompts the intern to raise the issue of full-time employment with the sponsor. In addition, this type of evaluation pinpoints problems early in the internship and allows supervisory personnel or faculty to take remedial action.

Student Perceptions of the Internship Course Content

Another technique of student evaluation is to look at the internship course itself. How was the course designed and implemented? Did the course syllabus accurately reflect actual course operations? Did you receive supervisory assistance as promised? How does the internship class compare with other academic offerings in the paralegal curriculum? Form 7-4 addresses these and other questions involving course content, as well as suggestions for improvement.

Form 7-4[3]

Intern Name_____Date_____

Internship Course Evaluation

Student Name_____ Number of courses completed in the paralegal program? _____
Placement Firm Name _____

1. What "learned" skills from courses taken as part of the paralegal program were most useful in your placement?
2. What new skills did you learn in your placement?
3. Describe what you learned about the attorney/legal assistant working relationship.
4. Describe what you learned about the attorney/client relationship (if applicable to your placement).
5. Was taking field studies at this particular point in your course work a good decision, or would you prefer to have done it earlier or later?
6. Has this field experience helped you reach a decision on what type of paralegal you wish to become? (e.g., legal specialty area? office size?)
7. How is field experience different from other classes in the paralegal program?
8. How has field experience influenced your feelings about the paralegal field as a career?
9. Were monthly seminars helpful in terms of
    a. providing information on the working world of paralegals?
    b. providing an opportunity for the interchange of ideas with other students?
10. What topics or general areas of discussion would have been helpful that were not discussed in the monthly seminars?
11. What could be added to the curriculum to better prepare students for their field experience?

CHAPTER 7

Student Perceptions of the Supervisor/ Sponsor

Your perception of your supervisor or sponsor should now be gauged. Was the supervisor accessible? Did the sponsor give sufficient explanation of your duties and responsibilities? How would you rate the supervisor as a mentor and guide through the dynamics of the internship? See Form 7-5.

Form 7-5

Intern Name_____Date_____

Evaluation of Supervisor/Sponsor

1. In what way did the supervisor help prepare you for your role as an intern?
2. Are there other things you would recommend that the supervisor should do to help prepare you for your role as intern?
3. Was your relationship with the field supervisor made clear to you? If so, how would you describe that relationship?
4. Could that relationship be improved in any way for the benefit of the intern? If so, how?
5. Did you and your supervisor develop a clear set of expectations regarding the activities that were to be included in the experience? If so, were these expectations delineated in the form of a contract?
6. If a contract was developed, did you find it to be useful? If so, how? If not, why not?
7. What supervisory activities did not prove to be very helpful to you?
8. What supervisory activities were particularly helpful for you?
9. Did your supervisor participate in your evaluation? If so, what was his/her role?
10. What intrinsic rewards do you feel your supervisor received from being an intern site supervisor?
11. Are there other rewards that you think your supervisor should be provided for acting as site supervisor? If so, please specify.
12. Do you think it would be useful for site supervisors to have opportunities to meet with other site supervisors? If so, about how frequently, and what do you think should happen at such meetings?
13. Would you recommend that we use your site supervisor again? Why or why not?
14. Do you have specific suggestions for improving the program? We are particularly interested in any thoughts you may have about the field experience and the role of your site supervisor.
15. Any other comments about the quality of supervision?

Student Perceptions of the Internship Location

Finally, your conclusions about the intership site — whether a law firm, agency, or business entity — should be solicited and cataloged. Institutions and faculty can decide whether or not the location is worthy of continued participation in the program.

EVALUATING
THE INTERNSHIP EXPERIENCE

Form 7-6 asks you to assess the firm or agency's performance. Through discussions with firm personnel and by reading the official publications of the firm, you should be aware of its goals and objectives by the end of your internship. The intern assessment should include a discussion of how well your firm meets its goals and objectives. The following questions are intended to guide you in your assessment:

1. How realistic are the firm's goals?
2. Which goals does the firm actually attempt to fulfill and which ones are merely for public relations?
3. What are some of the difficulties the firm faces in attaining its goals?[4]

Form 7-6

Intern Name_____Date_____

Evaluation of Internship Site

As part of our continued effort to improve our internship program, we would like your responses to the following questions. All responses will be kept confidential.

Please circle the number that most accurately reflects your service experience at your internship site.
1 = Poor 2 = Needs improvement 3 = Satisfactory 4 = Very good 5 = Excellent NB = No Basis

1. The firm provided training that was helpful and applicable.   1 2 3 4 5 NB
2. The firm provided clear explanations of their needs and goals.   1 2 3 4 5 NB
3. The firm provided clear explanations of your role and responsibilities.   1 2 3 4 5 NB
4. The firm's staff accepted you as a welcome addition to the staff.   1 2 3 4 5 NB
5. The firm provided sufficient feedback regarding your performance.   1 2 3 4 5 NB
6. The supervisor was accessible and visible.   1 2 3 4 5 NB
7. The service experience was meaningful and enjoyable.   1 2 3 4 5 NB
8. Would you recommend your placement site to another student? _____ Yes _____ No
9. Would you consider continuing serving at your current site? _____ Yes _____ No
10. Any comments about your internship site?

Sponsor/ Supervisor Evaluation of Intern

As an intern, you will be evaluated on two fronts: (1) the faculty evaluation and (2) the sponsor evaluation. In the former category, a faculty member or instructor is assigned to oversee your performance, acting as a bridge between your sponsor and your institution. The faculty member judges your performance by observing you in action and assimilates these observations with your sponsor's assessment of how you performed at the internship site.

CHAPTER 7

Faculty/
Instructor
Evaluation

The faculty member who acts as a conduit between the sponsor and the academic institution has a unique opportunity to see the intern in a dual light: in relation to the institution and in relation to the sponsor. Moreover, the faculty member is usually entrusted with the assessment of the intern's documentation and assignments for grading purposes. Review the Faculty Evaluation of Intern at Form 7-7.

Form 7-7

Faculty Evaluation of Intern

Student's Name:
Internship Location:
Supervisor's Name:

DAILY LOG
Content: (Do logs demonstrate a thoughtful analysis of the day?)
_____
_____

Completeness: (Were all logs present?)
_____

OVERALL GRADE:_____

FINAL REPORT
Content: (Does student demonstrate a thorough understanding of the paralegal profession? Are ethical dilemmas dealt with? Does the report demonstrate reflection on the experiences encountered?)
_____
_____
_____

Work Exhibits: _____
_____
_____

Format: (Proper spelling, spacing, footnotes, overall appearance?)
_____
_____

OVERALL GRADE:_____
Daily Logs:_____ Final Report:_____
Sponsor's Evaluation:_____ FINAL GRADE:_____
Faculty Supervisor _____ Date _____

EVALUATING
THE INTERNSHIP EXPERIENCE

Sponsor's Evaluation of Intern

As an intern, the recommendation crafted by your supervisor is a win or lose situation. Many faculty heavily weigh the sponsor's view, since it is the sponsor who works with you on a daily basis. It is the sponsor who appreciates the contributions you make and the challenges you meet. The following criteria of evaluation are best handled by the sponsor:

- performance as an employee
- performance on assignments
- professionalism and ethical behavior
- ability to work with others
- potential for employment as a paralegal.

Midterm Evaluation of Intern's Performance

Many institutions request a supervisory midterm evaluation of an intern's performance. This keeps the faculty members charged with the internship, and keeps the institution itself aware of the positive and negative aspects of the intern's performance early in the process. A few institutions may solicit feedback during the first week of internship activity, but more typical is a midterm evaluation tool like Form 7-8 on the following page.

CHAPTER 7

Form 7-8

Midterm Evaluation

Sponsor: Please complete this form after the first 10 hours of the internship.

Date:	Name of Sponsor/Supervisor (print):
Intern:	Signature of Sponsor/Supervisor :

1. Have any duties changed significantly since the internship was authorized?	Yes____ No____
If yes, please list them in comments section below.	
2. Is the Intern adjusting well to your office environment?	Yes____ No____
If no, please explain in comments section below.	
3. Does the Intern follow directions?	Yes____ No____
If no, please explain in comments section below.	
4. Have you met with the Intern to review progress to date?	Yes____ No____
If no, kindly schedule a meeting soon.	
5. Do you foresee any reason(s) why the Intern will be unable to demonstrate sufficient competence to earn academic credit for the internship?	Yes____ No____
If yes, please call our office at your earliest convenience.	

6. Please note any comments, questions, or suggestions below:

_____

_____

_____

_____

_____

_____

_____

_____

Thank you for taking the time to complete this form. Please mail, fax, E-mail, or phone in your responses to: _____

178

EVALUATING
THE INTERNSHIP EXPERIENCE

Final
Evaluation

The comprehensive nature of the final evaluation is obvious when compared to the preventive nature of the midterm review. At this stage, the game is over, impressions are solidified, tasks are completed, and the intern is discharged from further responsibilities. By this time, the sponsor sees the intern *in toto*.

Faculty members or educational institutions generally solicit a formal final sponsor report similar to Form 7-9. It contains questions on

- the intern's skill level
- areas for improvement
- strengths and weaknesses
- level of contribution
- personal work habits.

Form 7-9[5]

Evaluation of Field Studies

Student: Date:
Office or Agency:
Supervisor: Title:

1. Please list the skills learned and abilities demonstrated by this student during the semester.

    _____

    _____

2. Based on the above list, which areas are in need of improvement? Please indicate any weaknesses and how the student might improve.

    _____

    _____

3. Based on the above list, please indicate the student's strengths and how they were demonstrated.

    _____

    _____

4. Describe the overall contribution that the student made to your office.

    _____

    _____

5. May this student use your name as a reference for employment as a paralegal?

    _____

    _____

CHAPTER 7

Form 7-9 (continued)

6. Please use the following scale to evaluate the student in the following areas: (If any of the following do not apply, please omit.)

1 = Excellent
2 = Good
3 = Satisfactory
4 = Needs Improvement

1. DEPENDABILITY	1 2 3 4
2. EFFECTIVENESS	1 2 3 4
3. RESPONSIBILITY	1 2 3 4
4. FLEXIBILITY	1 2 3 4
5. COMMUNICATION SKILLS: WRITTEN	1 2 3 4
6. COMMUNICATION SKILLS: ORAL	1 2 3 4
7. ATTITUDE TOWARD RESEARCH	1 2 3 4
8. RESPONSIVENESS TO SUGGESTIONS AND CONSTRUCTIVE CRITICISM	1 2 3 4
9. HELPFULNESS TO ATTORNEY AND OFFICE	1 2 3 4
10. ORGANIZATION	1 2 3 4
11. ABILITY TO WORK WITH STAFF	1 2 3 4
12. ABILITY TO WORK WITH CLIENTS	1 2 3 4
13. UNDERSTANDING OF LEGAL CONCEPTS	1 2 3 4
14. APPLICATION OF LEGAL CONCEPTS	1 2 3 4
15. ABILITY TO SOLVE PROBLEMS	1 2 3 4
16. INITIATIVE	1 2 3 4

How would you rate this student's overall effectiveness?
EXCELLENT _____   GOOD_____   SATISFACTORY _____   NEEDS IMPROVEMENT _____
Date of Evaluation _____
Supervisor _____
Student _____
(Signature indicates that this evaluation was discussed with student.)

RETURN THIS FORM TO _____

A second format tends to integrate institutional measures of performance by listing a grading scale and a review of assignments such as logs and particular projects. See Form 7-10 on the following page.

EVALUATING
THE INTERNSHIP EXPERIENCE

Form 7-10

Sponsor's Evaluation

Student Name _____

Firm/Organization _____

Supervisor _____

Grading Scale:

97-100	A+
94 - 96	A
90 - 93	A-
87 - 89	B+
84 - 86	B
80 - 83	B-
77 - 79	C+
74 - 76	C
70 - 73	C-
67 - 69	D+
64 - 66	D
60 - 63	D-
59 or below	F

Please grade the student's performance in each of the following areas:

PERSONAL CHARACTERISTICS

Professional appearance _____

Receptiveness to evaluation and feedback _____

Oral communication _____

Written communication _____

Disposition _____

Punctuality _____

Maturity _____

Dependability _____

Responsibility _____

Effectiveness _____

Comments: _____

_____

_____

(continued)

CHAPTER 7

Form 7-10 (continued)

PROFESSIONAL CHARACTERISTICS
Relating to staff _____
Helpfulness to attorney _____
Ability to understand legal _____
Ability to apply legal concepts _____
Willingness to accept delegation of new or different responsibility _____
Comments: _____
_____
_____

PROJECT/QUALITY OF WORK
Writing skill _____
Planning of project_____
Initiative _____
Value to the office _____
Accuracy and thoroughness of work _____
Comments: _____
_____
_____

INTERNSHIP DAILY LOG
Accuracy _____
Organization _____
Thoroughness _____
Comments: _____
_____
_____

Please assign a numerical grade to the internship, using the grading scale on page 1 of Form 7-10. (Note: Student must earn a grade of 70% or higher in order to pass the internship course.)

Numerical Grade _____%

EVALUATING
THE INTERNSHIP EXPERIENCE

Form 7-10 (continued)

Overall Performance of the Student:
1. Have you hired this intern for a permanent position? Yes_____   No_____
2. Would you like to sponsor another intern from the Institute? Yes_____No_____ Maybe_____
   with the following conditions: _____
   If yes, when would you like the new intern to begin?_____
3. Did the intern have the paralegal skill/knowledge base required to perform entry-level tasks?
   Yes____ No _____
4. Were you satisfied with this intern's work performance? Yes ____ No_____
5. How would you suggest we improve our paralegal training program? _____
_____

Other Comments:_____
_____
_____

We greatly appreciate your participation in the internship program.

Sponsor Signature: _____ Date: _____
Student Signature: _____ Date: _____

Note to Sponsor: Please return the completed, signed Evaluation Form directly to _____ .

The preceding sample effectively differentiates categories that measure the complete paralegal, from personal traits to professional attributes and suitability for long-term employment.

A third approach to sponsor analysis is the Internship Evaluation in Form 7-11. In contrast to the other designs thus far, this evaluation asks the reviewer to write out a narrative describing the intern's experience.

Form 7-11

Evaluation of Internship

TO: Supervisory Personnel
FROM: _____
Please use the rating scale below to critically evaluate your assigned intern. Reports are due twice each semester. Contact me to determine filing times.

CHAPTER 7

Form 7-11 (continued)

Rating Scale:
1 = Excellent
2 = Good
3 = Fair
4 = Poor

___ 1. Punctuality
___ 2. Understanding of job requirements
___ 3. Willingness to listen to instructions
___ 4. Capacity to interact with others
___ 5. Adherence to rules and regulations
___ 6. Professional demeanor
___ 7. Conduct and behavior
___ 8. Quality of work
___ 9. Level of achievement (compared to others)
___ 10. Initiative
___ 11. Attention to instruction
___ 12. Leadership qualities
___ 13. Capacity to handle multiple problems
___ 14. General attitude
___ 15. Creative and innovative thinking

COMMENTS: Please give a two- or three-paragraph description of the intern, outlining both strengths and weaknesses and stating whether or not you would recommend the intern for an equal or similar position or would find him/her desirable as an employee.

Thank you so much for your kind assistance.

Sponsor Signature:_____ Date: _____
Student Signature: _____ Date: _____

When the sponsor must author an exposition of the intern, as in Form 7-11, there is an opportunity for a more personal critique not seen in quantitative measures like, "1 through 5," or "Excellent to Poor." Students tend to prefer the narrative style, because this type of documentation serves as a living recommendation.

EVALUATING
THE INTERNSHIP EXPERIENCE

Placement   Most interns hope to attain a full-time position as a paralegal after the internship
Readiness   is completed. Conduct a job-readiness inventory to see what you think about the
likelihood of your getting a placement. See Form 7-12.

Form 7-12

Intern Name_____Date_____

Inventory of Readiness for Job Placement

Topics	Degree of Readiness
1. Requirements completed for job qualifications.	1 2 3 4 5
2. Occupation preference clear.	1 2 3 4 5
3. Geographical preference clear.	1 2 3 4 5
4. Able to obtain good recommendations from administrators and professors.	1 2 3 4 5
5. Good sense of job market.	1 2 3 4 5
6. Good interviewing skills.	1 2 3 4 5
7. Resume developed, critiqued, and up to date.	1 2 3 4 5
8. Sufficient networks.	1 2 3 4 5
9. Sponsorship established with legal community.	1 2 3 4 5

Now that the internship is completed, you must express gratitude to those who
made it all possible. Even more important, placement offices, educational
institutions, and internship coordinators should thank the sponsor.
See Figure 7-1.

Figure 7-1[8]

Thank-You Letter to Sponsor from School

Dear _____ ,

Thank you for participating in the internship program by sponsoring _____
(student's name).

WE ARE VERY PROUD OF OUR PROGRAM AND OUR GRADUATES!! We hope that you will
continue to help us by assisting our graduates in their search for meaningful law-related employment.
Please contact me if you are interested in sponsoring another intern, if you would like to review
candidates for current or future job openings, or if you are able to serve as a referral to our colleagues in
your community.

Please note that all intern and employment referrals are made at no charge to either you or to our
students; these services are one component of our Placement Assistance Program.

CHAPTER 7

Figure 7–1 (continued)

Once again, thank you for your participation in our internship program. You provided _____ (student's name) with an invaluable opportunity to gain law-related work experience.

Sincerely,

Placement Director

Interns should correspond with both the faculty member and the sponsor. Letters like these generate enormous goodwill. See Figures 7-2 and 7-3.

Figure 7–2

Thank-You Letter to Sponsor from the Intern

Dear _____ :

Thank you for the wonderful opportunity to serve as an intern. The practical education I received from you and everyone else in the office was beyond comparison. I am now able to perform more paralegal functions correctly and confidently. I was given the constructive criticism I asked for. I had the chance to improve the skills that I lacked, with advice from all.

Thank you again! I will keep you posted on my employment status.

With warm regards,

[Intern's Name]

EVALUATING
THE INTERNSHIP EXPERIENCE

Figure 7-3

Thank-You Letter to the Faculty Supervisor from the Intern

Dear _____ ,

Now that my internship is complete, I want to thank you for all the support and guidance you gave to me. Your constructive criticism was highly valued and your suggestions for improvement were most effective. Thank you for the career advice. It proved most useful in my job search, as did the interview tips.

Thank you. I will keep you apprised of my employment status.

With warm regards,

[Student's Name]

Whether the experience of the internship will have long-term relevancy cannot be proved in the classroom. The intern will only sense the internship's efficacy in subsequent employment — full-time and permanent in nature. It is here that the reality of the internship either fits or balks at the reality of employment.

Select institutions survey their alumni to determine the impact of their internship programs. See Form 7-13 on the following page for a representative survey that elicits opinions on

- the quality of curricula
- the strength or lack of strength of the internship
- the type of position eventually attained
- whether the internship helped direct the choice of a position
- ease or burden of being in the internship program
- who and what types of positions were helpful to you
- suggestions for improvement.

187

CHAPTER 7

Form 7-13

Intern Name_____Date_____

Student Evaluation

It is important for the Paralegal Department to hear from paralegals who have completed their internships. Our ability to enhance and improve the program is dependent on your feedback. Please help us by taking the time to think about and complete this evaluation form.

I. Program Content

1. Please list and rate those courses that you have taken as part of the program:

Course No.	Course Title	Not Useful			Useful
_____	_____	1	2	3	4
_____	_____	1	2	3	4
_____	_____	1	2	3	4

(list all courses)

2. Which courses have you found most useful in preparing you for your career as a paralegal? _____
_____

3. Were there any courses you would delete or add to the program?
   Delete   Add

_____   _____
_____   _____
_____   _____

4. Please rate the following aspects of your internship program:
   Scale: W = Weak aspect
                 A = Acceptable aspect
                 S = Strong aspect

_____ Academic coursework   _____ Internship seminar
_____ Supervisor's input   _____ Administrator's input

EVALUATING
THE INTERNSHIP EXPERIENCE

Form 7-13 (continued)

5. Did you find any of the following to be a problem during the program?

	Not a problem			A major problem
Adding new roles	1	2	3	4
Time frame of the program	1	2	3	4
Site sponsor's exceptions	1	2	3	4
Home/personal responsibilities	1	2	3	4
Number of courses included in program	1	2	3	4
Faculty and curricula exceptions	1	2	3	4
Travel expectations	1	2	3	4
Other: _____	1	2	3	4

II. Networking and Cohort Development

6. Did you find that your fellow interns were helpful to you in dealing with the intensity of the internship experience?

____ Very helpful   ____ Somewhat helpful   ____ Not very helpful

7. Have you maintained contact with other interns?

_____ Yes _____No

III. Status Regarding a Paralegal Position

8. Have you applied for a paralegal position?

_____ Yes _____No

9. If you sought a paralegal position, when did you first do so?

___Immediately after the program   ___A year after the program
___Other: _____

10. If you sought a position, were you successful?

_____ Yes _____No

11. If you were successful, what is your role? _____

12. If you have not yet obtained a paralegal position, how much time are you willing to devote to obtaining such a position?

_____ None; I've decided I don't want to do so   ____ None; I don't believe I can obtain one
_____ For another year or two   ____ Five years maximum
_____ Until I get one   ____ Other:

CHAPTER 7

Form 7-13 (continued)

IV. Personal Issues

13. Was there a financial loss during the program?
_____ Yes _____No

14. Did you find that you had a good support network to help you get through the program?
_____ Yes _____No

15. Who formed the most important foundations of your support network?

	Not important			Very Important
Intern staff	1	2	3	4
Colleagues at school/agency	1	2	3	4
Other interns	1	2	3	4
Friends	1	2	3	4
Significant others	1	2	3	4

V. Outcome

16. Overall, how would you rate the program?
Not worth the effort   1   2   3   4   Highly worthwhile

17. Would you do it again, knowing what you know now?
_____ Yes _____No

18. Please give any advice or comments that will help us improve the internship program.

_____
_____
_____

Conclusion

Serving as an intern is one of the best ways to become oriented to the "real" legal world. As you become familiar with office environments, you will discover what type of practice appeals to you and what size office is the most comfortable. You will benefit not only through your own internship experience, but also through sharing information with your fellow students.

Through your internship you will learn what law firms and corporations want. Although these expectations may vary from firm to firm, all firms will expect the following:

EVALUATING
THE INTERNSHIP EXPERIENCE

1. written documents without errors
2. getting along well with attorneys and staff
3. competencies in your specialties and the ability to "hit the ground running."

The amount of involvement by school program directors will vary also. If your school leaves developing your internship to you, you will have an opportunity to take the initiative and plan your own internship program. This book will guide you through the process.

Whether you plan your own internship or follow your school's program, the experience will be invaluable. It will provide the best opportunity to determine your own goals, polish your skills, and search for the job just right for you. Think ahead to where you ultimately would like to work, and tomorrow's decisions will flow more easily.

Endnotes

1. American Institute for Paralegal Studies, Inc., Southfield, MI 48075.
2. San Francisco State University Paralegal Studies Certificate Program, San Francisco, CA 94132.
3. Gary R. Gordon and R. Bruce McBride, *Criminal Justice Internships*, 107, 2d ed., (1990).
4. San Francisco State University Paralegal Studies Certificate Program, San Francisco, CA 94132.
5. American Institute for Paralegal Studies, Inc., Southfield, MI 48075.
6. Waynesburg College Public Service Administration Program, Waynesburg, PA 15370.
7. American Institute for Paralegal Studies, Inc., Southfield, MI 48075.
8. American Institute for Paralegal Studies, Inc., Southfield, MI 48075.

CHAPTER 7

APPENDICES

APPENDIX A STATE CIVIL SERVICE CENTERS

ALABAMA
Personnel Department
64 North Union
Montgomery, AL 36130

ALASKA
Department of Administration
Division of Personnel
Pouch C-0201
Juneau, AK 99811

ARIZONA
Department of Administration
Personnel Division
1831 West Jefferson
Phoenix, AZ 85007

ARKANSAS
Department of Finance & Administration
Office of Personnel Management
P.O. Box 3278
Little Rock, AR 72203

CALIFORNIA
State Personnel Board
801 Capitol Mall
Sacramento, CA 95814

COLORADO
Department of Personnel
State Personnel Board
1313 Sherman Street
Denver, CO 80203

CONNECTICUT
Personnel Division
Department of Administrative Services
P.O. Box 806
Hartford, CT 06115

APPENDICES

DELAWARE
State Personnel Office
Townsend Building
P.O. Box 1401
Dover, DE 19901

DISTRICT OF COLUMBIA
D.C. Personnel Office
613 G. Street NW
Washington, DC 20001

FLORIDA
Department of Administration
Room 530, Carlton Building
Tallahassee, FL 32301

GEORGIA
State Merit System of Personnel Administration
200 Piedmont Avenue
Atlanta, GA 30334

GUAM
Office of Attorney General
7th Floor, Pacific News Building
Agana, GU 96910

HAWAII
Department of Personnel Services
830 Punchbowl Street
Honolulu, HI 96813

IDAHO
Personnel Commission
700 West State
Boise, ID 83720

ILLINOIS
State Civil Service Commission
425 1/2 S. Fourth Street
Springfield, IL 62701

APPENDICES

INDIANA
State Personnel Department
Room 513, State Office Board
100 North Senate Avenue
Indianapolis, IN 46204

IOWA
Merit Employment Department
Grimes State Office Board
East 14th & Grand
Des Moines, IA 50319

KANSAS
Department of Administration
Division of Personnel Services
State Office Building
Topeka, KS 66612

KENTUCKY
Department of Personnel
Capitol Annex
Frankfort, KY 40601

LOUISIANA
Department of Personnel
P.O. Box 44111
Capitol Station
Baton Rouge, LA 70804

MAINE
Department of Civil Services
State Office Building
State House Station 4
Augusta, ME 04333

MARYLAND
Department of Personnel
301 West Preston Street
Baltimore, MD 21201

APPENDICES

MASSACHUSETTS
Civil Service Commission
1 Ashburton Place
Boston, MA 02108

MICHIGAN
Department of Civil Sevices
Lewis Cass Building
320 S. Walnut St.
Box 30002
Lansing, MI 48909

MINNESOTA
Department of Employee Relations
3rd Floor, Space Center
444 LaFayette Road
St. Paul, MN 55101

MONTANA
Department of Administration
Personnel Division
Mitchell Building, Room 130
Helena, MT 59601

NEBRASKA
Department of Personnel
Box 94905
Lincoln, NB 68509

NEW HAMPSHIRE
Department of Personnel
State House Annex
Room 1
Concord, NH 03301

NEW JERSEY
Department of Civil Services
Division of Classification
East State & Montgomery Streets
CN 310
Trenton, NJ 08625

APPENDICES

NEW MEXICO
State Personnel Offfice
130 South Capitol
Sante Fe, NM 87501

NEW YORK
Department of Civil Services
State Office Building Campus
Albany, NY 12239

NORTH CAROLINA
Office of State Personnel
116 West Jones Street
Raleigh, NC 27611

NORTH DAKOTA
Personnel Office
1000 Eeast Divide Avenue
Box 1537
Bismarck, ND 58502

OHIO
Department of Administrative Services
Divisionof Personnel
30 East Broad St.
Columbus, OH 43215

OREGON
Executive Department
Personnel Division
155 Cottage Street NE
Salem, OR 97310

PENNSYLVANIA
Office of Administration
517 Finance Building
Bureau of Personnel
Harrisburg, PA 17120

SOUTH CAROLINA
Budget & Control Board
Division of Human Resource Management
1205 Pendleton Street
P.O. Box 12547
Columbia, SC 29211

APPENDICES

TENNESSEE
Departmentof Personnel
1st Floor, J.K. Polk Building
505 Deaderick Street
Nashville, TN 37219

TEXAS
Attorney General of Texas
Supreme Court Building
Austin, TX 78711

VERMONT
Agency of Administration
Department of Personnel
110 State Street
Montpelier, VT 05602

WASHINGTON
State Department of Personnel
P.O. Box 1789
Olympia, WA 98504

WEST VIRGINIA
Civil Service System
1900 Washington Street
East Room B-456
Charleston, WV 25305

WISCONSIN
Department of Employee Relations
149 East Wilson Street
P.O. Box 7855
Madison, WI 53707

APPENDICES

APPENDIX B   ANSWERS TO ETHICAL QUERIES (in Chapter Four)

Exercise #1: The Paralegal Fee
Answer: Yes. See *ABA Model Guidelines for the Use of Legal Assistants* 8-9:
8. A lawyer may include a charge for the work performed by a legal assistant in setting a charge for legal services.
9. A lawyer may not split legal fees with a legal assistant nor pay a legal assistant for the referral of legal business. A lawyer may compensate a legal assistant based on the quantity of the legal assistant's work and the value of that work to a law practice, but the legal assistant's compensation may not be contingent, by advance agreement, upon the profitability of the lawyer's practice.

Exercise #2: Confidences
Answer: Yes. See *NFPA Model Code of Ethics and Professional Responsibility*, at Canon 5.

Exercise #3: Unauthorized Practice of Law
Answer: Yes. See *NFPA Model Code of Ethics and Professional Responsibility*, at Canon 7.

Exercise #4: Fee Agreements
Answer: No. See *NALA Model Standards and Guidelines for Utilization of Legal Assistants*, Should not at 1

Exercise #5: Competency
Answer: Yes. See *NALA Code of Ethics and Professional Responsibility*, at Canon 5: A legal assistant must act prudently in determining the extent to which a client may be assisted without the presence of a lawyer.

Exercise #6: Disclosure of Paralegal Status
Answer: Yes. See *NALA Code of Ethics and Professional Responsibility*, at Canon 6: A legal assistant shall not engage in the unauthorized practice of law and shall assist in preventing the unauthorized practice of law.

Exercise #7: Lawyer and Paralegal Liability
Answer: No. See *NALA Code of Ethics and Professional Responsibility*, at Canon 1: A legal assistant shall not perform any of the duties that only lawyers may perform nor do things that lawyers themselves may not do.

APPENDICES

Exercise #8: Advertising
Answer: Yes. See *ABA Model Guidelines for the Use of Legal Assistants* 5: A lawyer may identify legal assistants by name and title on the lawyer's letterhead and on business cards identifying the lawyer's firm.

Exercise #9: Conflicts of Interest
Answer: Yes. See *ABA Model Guidelines for the Use of Legal Assistants* 7: A lawyer should take reasonable measures to prevent conflicts of interests resulting from a legal assistant's other employment or interests insofar as such other employment or interest would present a conflict of interest if it were that of the lawyer.

Exercise # 10: Lawyer Supervision
Answer: No. See *ABA Model Guidelines for the Use of Legal Assistants* 1: A lawyer is responsible for all of the professional actions of a legal assistant performing legal assistant services at the lawyer's direction and should take reasonable measures to ensure that the legal assistant's conduct is consistent with the lawyer's obligations under the *ABA Model Rules of Professional Conduct*.